The Found Dogs
The fates and fortunes of Michael Vick's pit bulls,
10 years after their heroic rescue

by Jim Gorant
New York Times Bestselling Author of
The Lost Dogs and *Wallace*

Front cover photo: Ashley Clark   *Back cover photo: Rachel Johnson*

PART I
The Trees

Time had not done much to contradict my memories. The farm fields still stretched along the sides of Virginia's Old State Highway 10. The whitewashed gas station still stood peeling in sun. And the turnoff to the little street remained nearly invisible among a stand of trees. Once found, the road's curbless, winding blacktop stretched out past the houses and fields. Until, finally, the white clapboard church rose on the right, directly across from the white-brick house set against the trees.

In the seven years since I'd visited 1915 Moonlight Road, the home of Bad Newz Kennels, very little had changed, yet something was clearly different. The place had first come into the public consciousness on April 27, 2007, when law enforcement officials executing a drug warrant uncovered evidence of a dog-fighting ring. A subsequent search led them to uncover 66 dogs, 51 one of which were pit-bull types thought to be key to the operation. As the dogs were removed from the property, news choppers hovered overhead, capturing images of the scared and thin animals being led out from beyond the four outbuildings—painted black from top to bottom, including the windows—hidden in the woods behind the house.

I pulled into the church lot and parked, gazing across the road at the house. The white iron fence looked the same, but gone were the ribbons of yellow police tape that read DO NOT CROSS. Gone were the red-and-white signs that said NO TRESPASSING, ANYONE CAUGHT ON THE PROPERTY WILL BE ARRESTED. The grass seemed a little greener, the landscaping refreshed and blooming. A new sign, a permanent one, mounted on the fence told the difference:

GOOD NEWS REHAB CENTER
FOR CHAINED AND PENNED DOGS

It was April 30, 2016, almost nine years to the day after that original raid, and I had been invited back for an event that was one-part reunion, one-part memorial, and one- part celebration. A check-in station sat just beyond the gate. A large white tent stood on the front lawn with a jumble of tables spread beneath. A few dozen people and a handful of dogs wandered around the grounds. I had stayed in touch with several of the people I'd gotten to know while writing *The Lost Dogs*, but I wasn't sure who would be here or what exactly to expect as I got out of the car and walked across the street.

• • •

Dogs Deserve Better is a non-profit rescue organization that started in 2002 with the aim of identifying pets that spent significant portions of their lives outside, either tied up or in pens. The group's volunteers would approach the owners and try to persuade them to change the way they were treating their dogs or to give them up. Over time the mission and approach evolved. The group still focuses on chained, penned, and abused dogs, but it addresses the problem by advocating for legal protections, educating communities, offering "fencing" grants and financial support for veterinary care and spay/neuter of rescued dogs. There are branches in Nashville and northern Virginia and volunteers spread across the country.

In 2011, the group raised funds and bought Michael Vick's former house, turning the headquarters of Bad Newz Kennels into the HQ of Dogs Deserve Better. The grounds, once the site of so much canine fear and pain, became a sanctuary where rescued dogs are rehabilitated and taught to live in a house before being put up for adoption. Today, up to 20 dogs are sheltered in the house where Vick and his cronies plotted their dogfights, including several pooches that live in what used to be the master bedroom. After checking in I popped into the house, entering through the garage and emerging in the kitchen. A maze of doggie gates divided the space, toys squeaked from every corner, and a mop of leashes dangled from pegs. Pictures of each dog rescued from Bad Newz decorated the walls.

Outside again, I made my way toward the sheds that stood beyond the back gate. They were still surrounded by trees, although far fewer than in 2007. Part of the mission of the weekend was to let those who had adopted Bad Newz dogs and other guests see these sheds before they were torn down. They were a natural point of curiosity and many of the people on hand had gathered near them.

Among them were Roo and Clara Yori, who had adopted Hector, (I had written a book about another of their dogs, Wallace, a rescued pit bull who'd gone on to become a flying-disc world champion), and Jim Knorr, the USDA agent who, along with local deputy sheriff Bill Brinkman, had led the 2007 investigation. I had kept in touch with Knorr over the years, and it was good to see him. Within minutes he was leading me, the Yoris, and a handful of others on a tour through the sheds.

Knorr explained what the law enforcement agents had found and where. He pointed out the stalls in the infirmary, the scales, the exercise equipment. He noted where they had seen syringes and questionable mixtures. He led us up to the second floor of the main shed, where the dogfights had taken place and showed us where he'd cut out blood- stained pieces of the plywood floor to have forensics testing done on them.

The details were gruesome and troubling but the mood was not. Time had passed. The early-spring day spread warmth and sunshine through the entire compound. Also, the more emotional portion of the weekend had occurred the day before.

• • •

Beyond the sheds, the largest tract of the 15-acre property stretched out in a sort of trapezoid. When Vick owned the land it had been thick with trees, which had obscured many of the dogs, who were stashed in small pens or confined by heavy chains with only a ramshackle wooden box or half a plastic barrel as shelter.

Dogs Deserve Better had cleared the field, leaving a large meadow. For the anniversary they had purchased 51 dogwood trees, dug 51 holes, and inscribed 51 plaques with the names of each of the dogs rescued nine years earlier. The day before, April 29, the adopters had been allowed to plant their dog's tree.

For those who had already lost their dogs, the process functioned as a second goodbye, dredging up deep feelings of loss and remembrance. For those whose dogs were still alive, the tree burial foreshadowed a sadness to come. Adopter Catalina Stirling, who took in Sweet Jasmine, expressed yet another impact of attendance. Being there, walking those grounds, poking through those buildings, had made her dog's previous life real to Stirling. Yes, Stirling had seen and felt Jasmine's pain, the fear so debilitating that at first the animal could not even walk outside on her own to relieve herself. But now the actions that had so impacted Jasmine were made actual in a way they had never been before. The way the heat built brutally in the sheds in the late hours, the smell of the clay soil, the taunting promise of the blue afternoon, each brought the realities of Jasmine's earlier life home.

Other adopters expressed a range of emotions: anger, sadness, relief, anguish, triumph, contempt, gratitude. The group included Stacey Dubuc, who works at the SPCA of Monterey, which took in three of the dogs, had adopted Ginger. Kevin and Jacque Johnson, who both worked at Best Friends, the Utah sanctuary that had taken in 22 of the dogs, adopted Ray. Molly Gibb, who'd taken Alf; Rachel Johnson, who'd adopted Oscar; and the publicity-shy couple who'd given a home to Shadow. Most, in some way or another, felt closure.

• • •

On Saturday, when all 51 trees had been planted—along with one weeping cherry dedicated to the dogs that never made it out of Bad Newz Kennels—a short ceremony ensued. There were prayers and speeches, the most powerful of which came from Bill Brinkman's teenage daughter: She read a letter from her father, who has worked in Afghanistan since shortly after leaving his job in Surry County. Afterward we lounged at the tables under the tent, telling stories, eating cake. At least two different groups splintered off with plans to go to dinner.

Before heading out I stopped back inside the house to thank

the Dogs Deserve Better staff. I stood and watched a few of the resident dogs sleeping and playing in the rooms adjacent to the kitchen. I couldn't help but think of the dogs that had come before, one of which had actually made the return trip for the day's events.

Uba is a stout black dog with a white belly and a white line that runs down between his eyes and spreads over his snout like spilled milk. He had been quite young, probably less than a year old, when he was taken from Moonlight Road. He trotted around the grounds, greeting the many strangers who wanted to say hello.

His owner, Letti DeLittle, even took him into the sheds. He became excited in the main shed, the one with the fight pit. But he spent a lot of time sniffing around the medical shed, particularly one stall, which very well could have been where he was whelped and even raised.

"He was not at all unhappy" to be there, DeLittle says. "You have to remember, he was grabbed from the only home he'd ever known and put in a concrete [shelter] for six months. That was probably more traumatic." Because he was so young when he left the property, Uba probably hadn't experienced much of the harsher life some dogs led at Bad Newz, although DeLittle notes that the first time she put him on a doggie treadmill, to get some exercise, he knew exactly what to do.

Still, Uba's day at his former home summed up the greater triumph and meaning of the effort to save these dogs: They are able to live a life that is not defined by the evil visited upon them by others. Or as DeLittle put it: "This is where he's from, not who he is."

When she took Uba to stand in front of the tree that bore his name, he showed once and for all how completely he'd moved on. After sniffing around for a few seconds, he lifted his leg and peed.

• • •

PART II
The Dogs

At the end of 2007 and into early 2008, the U.S. government released the 48 remaining pit bulls from Bad Newz Kennels to a variety of rescue groups around the country. The dogs were classified in three groups: Foster (must live with experienced dog owners for a minimum of six months; after further evaluation, adoption is likely); Sanctuary 1 (needs a controlled environment; possibility of adoption); and Sanctuary 2 (likely needs lifetime care by trained professionals; lesser chance for adoption). Of the total, 22 went to Best Friends animal sanctuary in Utah and 14 went to California—10 to Bad Rap, a rescue and advocacy group in Oakland, three to SPCA of Monterey, and one to Our Pack in Los Gatos. Richmond (Va.) Animal League received four dogs, while Recycled Love in Baltimore and Georgia SPCA each got three. Animal Farm Foundation and Animal Rescue of Tidewater took in one each. Ten years later, here is how those 48 dogs have fared.

ALF

When Molly Gibb first met Alf, at the Virginia municipal shelter where he was being held while the government determined his fate, she could see that he was out of balance and moved inefficiently. "He was bug-eyed and displaying dissociative behavior," she says.

Months later Alf and two other dogs were signed over to the Richmond Animal League (RAL). Gibb, who lives in Oklahoma, had met then-RAL board member Sharon Corbett when the two were rescuing dogs in Louisiana after Hurricane Katrina. Gibb's family had been involved with pit bulls going back more than 100 years, as both working dogs and companions, and she had been a professional dog handler since 1996, taking on training, therapy, and search-and-rescue.

She was also a practitioner of Feldenkrais, a physical therapy method named after its founder, Moshe Feldenkrais, that purports to change the way people and animals think by altering the way they move. So when Alf arrived at her home months later, Gibb began to build trust by giving him choices, safe places, and plenty of contact. Since he liked other dogs, she always had a few around him. To get him into balance, she had him walking on planks, then on a full obstacle course, which also built confidence. She even used body wraps, which she says helps dogs get a sense of their physicality.

Before long the dog that had been "running around, buggy-eyed and afraid to engage," whose first instinct when approached was to lie flat like a pancake, started to come into his own. Alf's face softened. He began to interact more. And where he initially dreaded the car, he began to love going for a ride. He started to play. With the big ears that earned him his name flopping around, Alf became a goofy, fun-loving dog.

He had physical struggles, though. Gastrointestinal problems followed him from the outset and over time he had two surgeries. One day he got hold of a piece of rawhide. Gibb tried to get him to vomit it up but couldn't. She rushed Alf to the vet, who decided to keep him for observation. During the night he had a hemorrhage and died almost instantly.

That was September 2009, almost two years after he arrived. "I'd like to think we made the most of that time, however short," Gibb says. "He was a great teacher and a reminder to stay in and enjoy the present moment."

AUDIE

When I was writing *The Lost Dogs*, Audie was training for canine agility competition, in which dogs run through a series of gates and earn points by beating a standard time. Linda Chwistek, a Bad Rap volunteer who adopted Audie, had set up a short course in her Northern California yard and the two were making steady progress. But things got tougher when they joined a class. Audie's debilitating fear of other dogs and loud barking caused him to lose focus.

On a few occasions, Chwistek came close to quitting the class—Audie was so scared it didn't seem worth the effort. But each time, the other handlers talked her out of it and together brainstormed ways to make the sessions more comfortable for Audie. She stuck with the training.

After a year the two were at a competition when Audie was called up to the line. As Chwistek walked him out she noticed something different about her dog: He was focused and unconcerned. The race started and Audie took off. "He was just out running," Chwistek says, "and I knew we were finally there."

Eventually, Audie conquered his fear of other dogs, sharing a home with Sailor, a two-year-old pit bull who's beginning to do a little agility training, and Ida, a six-year-old shelter dog. He even helped Chwistek work with foster dogs she brought in over the years.

In 2015, Audie earned enough points to qualify for the 2015 AKC Nationals in Reno, which was Chwistek's goal for him. He retired from agility competition shortly after—he had ACL surgery—but began competing in nose work, a sport in which dogs race to track a scent over a large course. And, as he did when he first moved in with Chwistek, Audie frequented the local waterfront, where he visited with friends who plied him with treats.

In 2011 Dorothy Hinshaw Patent wrote a children's book about him, *Saving Audie,* and Chwistek brought it when she and he made appearances at public libraries to teach kids about responsible dog ownership. In front of the crowd Audie performed a wide range of tricks that Chwistek taught him. The kids liked the book, but they loved the fun-loving ham that Audie had become.

Although he appeared to be in good health, in late April of 2017, vets found tumors in Audie's lungs and shortly thereafter, he died.

BONITA

Bonita arrived at Best Friends with babesia, a parasitic infection carried in and transferred through the blood; scars on her face; and a mouth full of broken and filed teeth. The assumption was that she had been used as a bait dog, which, naturally, made her fearful. As she got a sense of her new surroundings, though, she was eager to make friends. With attentiveness and some positive feedback, she came around quickly, charming her handlers with a willing—if slightly crooked—smile. In short order she became a certified lap dog who loved to do tricks. But she continued to suffer dental problems, and in February 2009 she went in for surgery. She never came out of the anesthesia.

CHERRY GARCIA

Paul Fiacone and his fiancée, Melissa, were in the process of buying a house when he realized he needed to confess.

Years earlier, when the two were just dating, Fiacone had adopted a dog, Madison. Madison was a pit bull. That didn't mean much to Fiacone until he took his dog for a walk: Some people yelled at him, others avoided him. He began to understand the public had preconceptions about his sweet dog.

He was also a big NFL fan, so when the Vick case broke, he followed it closely. That included watching every episode of *Dogtown*, the National Geographic Channel show about the residents of Best Friends' canine facility. One episode featured a black dog from the Vick bust named Cherry Garcia, and despite his previous devotion to both Melissa and Madison, Fiacone admits that, "I fell for him.

"He was so shut down," Fiacone says, "that I just wanted to grab him and tell him everything will be okay."

As he lay in bed that night, he kept thinking about Cherry, about how Madison would make a great role model, about how the new house he and Melissa were buying would give the dog space and a safe yard. It all seemed to make sense. So he threw off the blankets, went to his computer and put in an application. The only thing he failed to do was discuss the plan with Melissa. When he finally fessed up, he concluded with what seemed all too obvious: "Don't worry, we have no shot."

That proved to be the only thing Fiacone was wrong about. Best Friends wrote back, not to say he had no shot but that Cherry wasn't yet ready to leave. A few months later Best Friends reached out to him. Cherry was still working on earning his Canine Good Citizen (CGC) certificate, which requires a dog to pass 10 temperament tests, but the organization wanted to initiate the long process of background checks, insurance verification, and home inspection. As each step progressed Paul and Melissa kept asking each other the same question: "Does this mean we're getting him?"

Finally, in August of 2009, the three of them—Fiacone, Melissa and Madison—flew out to Utah. When they walked into the room to meet Cherry, Madison trotted to the middle of the space, looked around, and plopped down on the floor. Cherry came over and sat right next to her. The quartet spent the next few days together without any sign of discord, and two weeks later Cherry arrived at the Fiacones' house.

And for two weeks after that, he didn't get off the couch. He had to have his food served to him there, and he had to be carried out to relieve himself. He slept with one eye open. At night, Paul and Melissa would hear him padding around, exploring under the cover of darkness, but in the morning, he'd once again be moored to the cushions.

Slowly they began moving his food bowl closer to the couch. He'd hop down, take a bite, and jump back up, and thus, slowly, he'd eat. Periodically, they'd move the bowl further away from the couch. It was eight months before he could eat normally.

Madison helped with his progress. She took on a mothering role and once he got off the sofa, he stuck to her like a bad reputation. She taught him how to live in a house, alternating between coddling and protecting him and encouraging him, at times all but physically pushing him through the doggy door. More important, Cherry saw how Madison interacted with the Fiacones and began to emulate her, which is how he built a relationship with them. The couple learned from him too. They saw how a regimented schedule helped him feel more secure, so they set a day-to-day plan and stuck with it.

At least they did until Roo Yori (who had adopted Hector) invited them and Cherry to attend a meet-and-greet event in Philadelphia. Fiacone was wary, but Yori convinced him everything would be okay. It wasn't. Cherry basically shut down and Fiacone feared he'd done some damage, maybe even set back the dog's progress. But back at home, the opposite happened. Cherry embraced his routine with new vigor, as if he now appreciated it more.

To push him a little, the Fiacones bought a big tub of treats and began rewarding Cherry any time he did something positive. At first he wouldn't take the goodies directly from their hands, but over time he grew more comfortable. Before long he'd walk up and bark for one. They started passing out the treats to strangers when they were out and Cherry would take them from anyone who offered. These days Cherry does five or six events a year at which he meets dozens of new people while promoting a positive image of pit bulls and responsible ownership.

That sort of resilience has become Cherry's trademark. When Madison passed away from liver cancer in 2015, Cherry dragged around for a few weeks, then moved on. By that point he also had Walker the cat to hang out with as well as the Fiacones' two kids. Last year, the family adopted a one-year-old pit bull named Eleanor Roosevelt, to whom Cherry has taken as well.

Perhaps even more impressive was Cherry's bounce back after leg surgery. He'd had the ACL in his back left leg repaired in 2009, but it never really got better and even began to deteriorate slowly. The situation grew so bad that he didn't even use the leg when he walked, and Fiacone could tell he was in pain. In July 2016, doctors amputated the leg. For the next 24 hours, Cherry struggled and Fiacone wondered if they'd made a mistake. But the following morning Cherry popped up and began tearing around the doctor's office. When he got home, he burst out of the doggy door, sprinted across the yard and lay down in the sun.

"That's what I love about him," Fiacone says. "No matter what happens, no matter what he's been through, he just keeps moving forward."

CURLY

A key moment in Cherry Garcia's recovery at Best Friends came when he started spending his days in the manager's office, hanging around with the people who worked there. This socialization helped Cherry so much that the staff soon let another of the dogs, Mya, join him. Since he knew the people and the routine, Cherry helped Mya relax.

When Cherry was adopted, Curly took his spot in the manager's office, and Mya became his mentor. Like Mya, he has come a long way since then, although he may never recover enough to leave Best Friends. That may be for the best, since Curly has allergies that require a special diet, and the trauma he endured still makes him afraid of strangers—of both the human and the canine variety. He's also unnerved by new places and open spaces.

When he does feel comfortable, though, he can be playful to the point of mischief. He loves being dressed up in garish red pajamas, and he's been known to pull things off desks and chew up boxes. He regularly jumps on operations manager Matt Fisher's desk to look out the window, knocking things down and making a general mess. In response Fisher has posted a CURLY FREE ZONE sign among his paperwork, although Curly frequently reminds everyone that he cannot read.

DENZEL and TUG

These two had much in common and an intertwined history. Both suffered from babesia, enduring occasional flare-ups that seemed to take a bit more out of them with each occurrence. Both were shy and frightened around people they didn't know and neither could really be around other dogs.

And both were involved in a still unexplained but fatal incident at Best Friends in October 2010. One night, Denzel, Tug and another dog not from the Vick pack, all broke out of their runs. Surveillance cameras did not pick up how this happened or what followed, but when the staff arrived in the morning both Denzel and Tug were injured and the other dog was dead. Best Friends was devastated by the tragedy, and in response the facility reinforced all the enclosures and instituted a night patrol.

Denzel and Tug lived out their lives without further incident and passed away within seven months of each other—Tug in June 2016 and Denzel in January 2017. Denzel, who was smart and had a penchant for learning tricks, including "waving" to visitors and balancing a large ball on his nose, loved running in the rain, splashing in the creek and going for walks. Tug, who was bigger, about 75 pounds, did everything at full speed, including riding shotgun around the sanctuary in a golf cart and taking running leaps into the laps of the people he loved. For those who knew him, that was his greatest impact.

ELLEN

She was the first of the Vick dogs at Best Friends allowed to spend time with outsiders, and she made a great ambassador. Sweet and friendly, she doled out kisses like a game show host. Once she was done licking she'd roll over for her favorite thing in the world—a good belly rub, a predilection that earned her the nickname Ellen Belly.

When she'd arrived at the sanctuary she could have gotten that name for another reason: She was overweight. With a better diet and exercise she trimmed down and made the most of her time. Although she didn't do well with other dogs, she cherished her interactions with people. In the end, though, gastronomic issues caught up with her. She began having trouble keeping on weight and digesting her food. As she slowly wasted away the staff ran through batteries of tests trying to identify the problem and find a solution, but to no avail. With no other options and no quality of life, this pioneer dog was put down in June 2012.

ERNIE

Sasha Best considers herself a failed foster. About the time the Bad Rap dogs arrived in Oakland, Best was enrolled in one of the group's training classes with her pit-bull mix, Hannah. Ernie was staying with a foster family, but they had a small house and he was a big dog. Bad Rap founders Donna Reynolds and Tim Racer asked Sasha and her husband if they would consider taking over the foster for one month, since they had more room and a half-acre fenced yard where the dogs could run. The Bests said yes.

When Ernie arrived, they set him up to succeed, giving him his own space and closely monitoring play when he interacted with Hannah and their two cats, especially the male, Henry, who ran the place. Ernie wasn't quite sure what to make of the cats, but he played with them even as he treated them with respect. With Hannah, he romped and jumped and ran like a pup. In all, Ernie seemed most concerned with figuring out what he was supposed to do, watching everyone carefully and reading the feedback he got—from people and animals—which helped him adjust quickly.

He had only one problem: He thought he was a lap dog, and at his size, he most definitely was not. Luckily, if he couldn't sit atop someone, he would happily roll onto his side and accept a belly rub. Ernie was turning out to be a great foster guest. Then Reynolds called: Someone had put in an application to adopt him.

Best's heart sank. She realized he belonged right where he was.

Nine years later, that is where he remains. Hannah and one of the cats are gone, but Ernie and Henry carry on.

Ernie sleeps on the Bests' bed at night, and he and Henry spend the day together, often curled up on the couch next to each other. On weekends he often goes on long hikes where he is allowed to simply follow his nose.

"He's the same dog he was when we got him," says Best. "Sweet and sensitive, a big, wonderful goofball."

FRODO

One of the more skittish dogs to go to Bad Rap, Frodo has acclimated to life in a house, although he still battles his demons. New people, new places and new experiences are upsetting. He won't walk on concrete sidewalks and loud noises overwhelm him. He follows his adopter, Kim Ramirez, around everywhere she goes and won't go to sleep at night until she does. Even then, he rests better with the radio on, a little white noise to drown out any scary, unfamiliar sounds.

Ramirez regularly takes Frodo for walks on wooded trails around her house to acclimate him to new places. Each new one is a challenge, so they'll start on a familiar path and slowly venture onto an unknown one. Frodo might initially make it half a mile on a strange route. But Ramirez will bring him back the next week and go a little farther. Then a little farther, and eventually Frodo will "conquer" another trail. With each successful outing, Ramirez says, he grows more confident.

Around the house, she has used the "touch" command to draw him out. When requested, he'll come and touch her hand with his nose. So when she gets, say, a fearsome new vacuum cleaner, she'll leave it in the middle of the room, stand a few feet away, and have him come touch her hand. Over subsequent days, she'll move a little closer each time, and slowly Frodo will grow more comfortable around the object. Eventually he'll be able to touch the actual vacuum.

Of course he also uses his nose nudges to indulge his impish side. He'll often bump the parrot cage to tease its inhabitant, and after dinner he'll approach the other two pit bulls that live in the house, Maggie and Doja, and give them playful pokes to get them to chase him. Frodo remains timid, but he's not afraid of having a little fun.

GEORGIA

One of the two known Grand Champion fighters in Vick's pack, Georgia arrived with a bad attitude and no teeth (they fell out on their own, for reasons no one has been able to explain). She growled, she guarded things, she refused to make eye contact. But she quickly figured out that the people at Best Friends were there to help. As it turned out, there was big personality hiding behind the snarl, a demeanor that Michelle Weaver, Best Friends' director of animal care, described as "you're going to love me."

Part of her appeal was the mix of goofy and gnarly she showed the world. She was covered with scars, but without her teeth her face was soft and foldy. Adding to the overall effect, she had broken her jaw at some point, which meant her mouth didn't close quite right and her tongue poked out. Perhaps that's why she became a media favorite, appearing in numerous photo spreads and making several television appearances, earning her the nickname Jet Set Diva.

Georgia loved playing, stuffed toys, running in a downpour, and dumping out her water bucket and wearing it on her head. She also loved puppies but only tolerated grown dogs, which was partly why she struggled to pass her CGC. When she finally did so in 2011, she was quickly adopted into a home where she was the only dog and unquestioned queen, a title she showed her appreciation for by doling out a steady supply of kisses. Late in 2013 she began to struggle with kidney disease, and eventually passed in December of that year.

GINGER

Ginger had some mass cell tumors removed in August 2016, but she's in generally good health and her graying coat is a reminder of how long she's been able to live a normal life. "It's been so long, I don't even think about [where she came from] anymore," says Stacy Dubuc, a manager at the SPCA of Monterey, who has had Ginger since 2008. "I just treat her like my dog."

That may be because Ginger has blended in from the start. She gets along well with Dubuc's two other dogs, looks forward to her five-plus-mile hikes on weekends— as long as it's not too hot—and enjoys snuggling up on the couch for a nap, although in some ways she remains a bit of a loner. On occasion she gets together for play sessions with fellow Vick refugee Stella, who lives nearby, but if Dubuc and the rest of the pack gather for a Sunday afternoon movie or are simply hanging around, Ginger is likely to seek out her crate in Dubuc's bedroom, which remains her safe haven. At night she moves to Dubuc's bed, where she tends to hog space and snore.

Ginger goes to Dubuc's office every day, where she starts the morning with a well-researched "tour of suckers," those people whom she knows have treats to give. Mission accomplished, she camps out under Dubuc's desk, occupying herself with her second-favorite pastime after eating: sleeping. Still, she recognizes the sound and cadence of approaching visitors, and if she hears someone she knows to carry goodies, she'll pop up to say hello.

Laughing a bit at the idea, Dubuc adds, "She's the best dog I could have wished for."

GRACE

In 2009 Susan* learned that her little black pit bull with a white spot, Bijou, had cancer. The vet told her that the dog had but a few months to live. Susan was heartbroken. She'd had Bijou since before she'd had her kids, the oldest of whom was approaching his teens. She knew she'd be desperate to get another dog right away.

She started looking, and partly because she lived in Northern California, her search led her to Bad Rap's website. There she found Grace, who was all white with a black spot. The symmetry was impossible to miss. She wrote to Bad Rap, wondering if Grace should be her next dog. The staff was open to exploring the possibility of Susan adopting Grace, though Susan wanted to wait until Bijou's time came before moving forward. Bad Rap was patient but cautioned her that if another adopter emerged they would pursue that option as well.

Bijou hung on for more than a year, allowing Susan to enjoy every minute she could get with her dear friend. After she took a little time to mourn, she returned to thoughts of her next dog and the Bad Rap website. To her surprise, she found that Grace was still available. Susan went to visit, hoping to figure out why. Was there something off or intimidating about the dog? Was she distant and traumatized?

Susan found no indications of anything like that. Grace was well-behaved and happy. Everywhere she'd gone the foster families had done their best to decompress and train her, and, Susan says, "We got the gift of their hard work."

Plus, Susan noticed, Grace "made this little warm face" that almost immediately sealed the deal. Within a few months, Grace had moved in and started her new life.

Susan, a nurse, began training Grace to become a hospital therapy dog. This turned out to be a great choice, because though Grace was selective about what dogs she wanted to play with, she loved people and particularly kids.

Whenever Grace and Susan arrived at the hospital, Grace would wiggle with excitement. Besides being friendly, she was one of those dogs who had a sense of people's feelings and seemed to be able to tell when someone was sick or sad. She behaved differently with different kids, clowning and performing for some and quietly snuggling with others.

After about a year, Susan and her family moved to Nevada, which meant Grace would have to get recertified to continue her therapy work. She had begun to slow down by then, and it also seemed to Susan that Grace grew weary more rapidly on each successive outing. She decided the therapy days were behind them.

After the move, Susan began to work at home, so now she and Grace spend the entire day together. They go for long walks every morning, often with Grace's best buddy, who lives nearby. The two dogs play and roughhouse happily, but Grace still has a well-attuned prey drive that causes her to dislike some dogs and sends her after rabbits, squirrels and even blowing leaves "from, like, zero to eighty in a nanosecond," according to Susan.

Then it's back home, where Grace spends the day lying near Susan or sleeping on the bed. As she looks back, Susan thinks that although it took a few stops and several years, Grace eventually fulfilled her destiny: "I feel like we let her be the dog she was supposed to be."

*Name withheld upon request.

GRACIE

After landing with Richmond Animal League board member Sharon Corbett, Gracie became "a local rock star," says her adopter, making a lot of appearances, doing tons of media and helping to change the perception about pit bulls. But she was also babesia positive. In the autumn of 2013 she started exhibiting symptoms of the disease, including disturbing digestive problems that her vets could never quite figure out.

The symptoms would disappear for long stretches, then she'd have bad episodes that drained her. Gracie began to slow down but retained her sweet nature. When Corbett brought home a small, abused beagle, one of five dogs in the house at the time, Gracie was the one who protected the beagle, making sure it felt safe.

By early 2015, Gracie's symptoms had become more persistent. One morning in January she was up early and needed to go out. Corbett escorted her; what Gracie produced was mostly blood. Corbett scooped her up and took her to the emergency center. As doctors discussed possible causes, Corbett looked at her dog. She could see that Gracie was tired and suffering. She knew it was time.

"As much as it hurt me, to keep her alive would have been selfish," she says.

But Gracie lives on in other ways. After she died, a group of volunteers and workers from the Richmond Animal League started Gracie's Guardians, which aims to improve the welfare of pit bulls in the Richmond area through outreach, education and spay-and-neutering programs. Specifically, the group goes into struggling parts of the area and makes connections with the community, engendering goodwill that softens the ground for their programs.

Corbett finds the accomplishments of Gracie's Guardians satisfying because the group continues to carry out what she always considered Gracie's mission. "The goal was to show society that they have nothing to fear from these dogs," she says. "She did her job."

HALLE

Heading into the start of 2007 Traci Madson knew who she was: a musician, a woman who worked at a fire station and a German shepherd person. The shepherd she owned at the time had long since retired from search-and-rescue work and his time was running out. Another German shepherd seemed the obvious choice for her next dog, although her new neighbors had this pit bull. At first Madson had been wary of it, but once she got to know the pooch she'd fallen in love. Maybe she should consider that type of dog?

That's how Madson found herself on the Best Friends website. "I'm not a sports person at all, so I had no idea who Michael Vick was," she says. "But when I read about those dogs it broke my heart." She volunteered to adopt one of the dogs, but none was yet ready. She called back every two weeks or so to check in and re-register her interest.

Finally, on one call, an adoption counselor told her that the Vick dogs were still not ready, but if she really wanted a pit bull they had one in the facility that was experiencing severe shelter stress. He'd begun chewing on his tail, to the point that they'd had to amputate. He needed a home.

Madson ended up adopting the dog, Tacoma. But she let Best Friends know she was still interested in a Vick dog.

In less than six months, a few of the dogs were ready. Since Best Friends knew Tacoma and knew the Vick dogs, Madson thought it might be best if the shelter suggested a good match. Her advisers recommended Halle, and shortly thereafter Madson and Tacoma drove to visit. The dogs hit it off, and Halle became the first of the Vick dogs at Best Friends to find a home.

As ready as she was, her adjustment was difficult. Unlike many of the other dogs Halle seemed to prefer big, open rooms and spaces, and she hated thresholds. Two months passed before she could walk on a leash. In order to help socialize Halle, Madson began bringing her to work. While Halle accepted treats from the firefighters who stopped by to visit, she would also get nervous and shake at times.

Other dogs posed no problem, though, especially Tacoma, and she seemed more secure when he was around. Everywhere she went, he went along, and that was an enormous help to her.

Yet Madson wanted more for her dog, so she hired a trainer and the two worked intensely with Halle for six months. By the end Halle had learned a lot, but so had Madson. She'd grown intrigued by the effort and began the process of getting her training certification.

Meanwhile, Halle continued to progress. Madson is in a band and gives music lessons. Early on, Halle was afraid of the instruments and went upstairs to hide during lessons or rehearsals. But by the third year or so, she began to hang around. Eventually, she'd come sit next to the kids taking their lessons and even solicit a little attention and petting.

Around that time, Madson adopted a third pit bull, Jagger, a small guy with a spinal injury. The three dogs were so inseparable and such a part of her life that when she left the fire station and opened her training business she called it Three Little Pits.

In 2015 Tacoma was diagnosed with lymphoma. The disease spread slowly but steadily, and eventually he had to have one leg amputated. About a year later Halle came up with a leg injury of her own. Madson took her to the vet, but the doctor hardly looked at her leg. Her nodes were swollen, "as big as hard-boiled eggs," Madson remembers him saying. Halle too had lymphoma, and hers progressed quickly. In October 2016, she was gone. Tacoma died three weeks later.

"They spent, basically, their whole lives together," Madson says. "And they changed the whole course of mine."

HANDSOME DAN

By the time *The Lost Dogs* went to press Dan had been adopted and sent off to his new home, but as part of Best Friends' agreement with the adopting families the group would not release names or contact numbers. The book made do with a description of Dan's life at Best Friends, but shortly after it came out I was friended on Facebook by his adopter, Heather Gutshall.

Gutshall, who lives in Rhode Island, started volunteering in shelters as a teen and was quickly drawn to the hardest cases: those dogs least likely to be adopted (because of behavior issues or age) and fight-bust survivors. After college she started a pet-care business, Outbound Hounds, that specialized in walking, sitting and providing day care for dogs, and she expanded it to include rescues, focusing on those hard cases. She followed the Vick situation closely, and when the call for adopters went out she filed an application, thinking to herself, "It will never happen." It happened.

Gutshall worked with personnel at Best Friends to find the right match. Finally, she flew to Utah to meet and bring home her new dog, Mel.

At the time, Mel was staying with a foster caregiver who lived a half-hour from Best Friends. While Gutshall waited for Mel and his foster to arrive, she was asked if she would like to meet Handsome Dan, the other dog she'd considered. After 15 minutes with Dan, she had the staff call Mel's foster and tell him to turn around. She was hooked. Why? "Dan was a mess," she says. "He had fear issues and was babesia positive, and I knew I was in a better position to deal with that than others would be."

She was right. She ran her business and her rescue out of her home, so she was always available to Dan. She had facilities for entertaining and caring for dogs and an ongoing, on-call relationship with a local veterinarian. After the pair made their way to Rhode Island, Gutshall promptly renamed her operation Handsome Dan's Rescue and promoted the undertaking's namesake to CCO, or Chief Canine Officer.

She also set about trying to calm Dan's fears and continue his progress toward a Canine Good Citizenship certificate. That particular project lasted about six months. "His biggest problem was walking on a loose leash," Gutshall says. "He would just pancake or tremble or pee." Sometimes he'd even do all three at once. Gutshall finally called Best Friends and told them a CGC for Dan wasn't going to happen. "I just felt it was inhumane to keep pushing him," she says.

She by no means gave up on Dan, though. She worked with him so intensely and with such dedication that in the ensuing years she became a certified trainer, then a certified behaviorist. Gutshall had a young daughter when she brought Dan home and now has a son as well. From the start Dan has gotten along well with kids. He's good with dogs and especially enjoys get-togethers with fellow Bad Newz survivor Cherry Garcia, who lives within driving distance.

Dan's now getting frail, so he doesn't play much with other dogs anymore, and the larger world still sets off his anxieties. But he can walk two or three houses up the street on leash, and he's comfortable and free in Gutshall's home. "If you saw him around the house you would never know," she says. That has been Handsome Dan's saving grace: He and Gutshall have spent every day together, which has made his life secure and pleasant. Hers too.

The benefits have compounded for other dogs as well. Because of his history Dan attracted a reliable cohort of donors to Gutshall's rescue operation, which has allowed her to save so many other hard cases. Says Gutshall: "We wouldn't have been able to do all of it without Dan's notoriety and the legacy of the Vick case."

HECTOR

After being transported from Virginia to California to Washington, back to California and then on to Minnesota, Hector finally found a home, but when he got there he was hardly the most famous pit bull in the house. His adopters, Roo and Clara Yori, already had Wallace, a high-energy, high-drive pittie who had struggled in a shelter—to the point that he was about to be put down—yet thrived in their home, winding up a world champion flying-disk catcher.

Hector and Wallace lived with four other dogs of various sizes and genders and their situation contained a certain irony: Wallace, an internationally known ambassador for the breed, was dog-reactive and couldn't really mingle with the other members of the pack, while Hector, the scarred veteran of a fight ring, got along great with the gang and spent many afternoons snoozing on the bed with Scooby and Mindy.

Soon after arriving Hector earned his therapy certification and made visits to hospitals, schools and senior centers. He also made TV appearances on CBS, PBS and E! Eventually, those visits slowed, as the Yoris felt that he'd done his job giving back and deserved to simply enjoy being a dog. At about that same time Wallace was diagnosed with a rare blood cancer. (This diagnosis came three weeks after *Wallace*, a book I'd written about his life, came out.)

Over the next year, the Yoris focused on Wallace, creating a bucket list for him and using social media to chronicle their efforts to help him check every box. They figured they would have time with the other dogs once Wallace's story had come to an end, which it did in September 2013.

A month later Hector fell ill and was eventually diagnosed with an aggressive form of cancer. The Yoris did everything they could to spoil him and ease his suffering.

He got acupuncture. He went for as many walks as he could handle, sometimes off leash. He received a steady diet of his favorite food: blueberry doughnuts.

He had spent the first two years of his life at Bad Newz and the seven years after in freedom, so toward the end the Yoris posted a picture of him wearing a sign that read: "Vick 2, Hector 7. I win." One follower of Hector's Facebook page saw the photo and sent a $7 donation. Others saw that and did the same, and the Yoris received a deluge of donations. They poured the money into the Wallace the Pit Bull Foundation, which they had started to contribute to rescue facilities, foster caregivers and programs aimed at helping homeless dogs.

When Hector finally passed, a little more than a year after Wallace, Roo, a college soccer player, found another way to honor his dogs. In 2016 he was accepted to compete on *American Ninja Warrior*. Appearing as the K9 Ninja, promoting animal adoption, he was highlighted on the show three times while progressing all the way to the finals. He was invited to compete again in 2017.

Giving back, and adopting a new pit bull, Johnny, has helped, but it doesn't mean it's been easy to let Hector go. "Every time I'm in the store and I see blueberry doughnuts," Yori says, "I think of him."

IGGY

When *The Lost Dogs* came out Nicole Rattay, the former Bad Rap volunteer, had moved to Southern California and started her own rescue called Just a Dog. Iggy, the most shut-down of the Bad Rap dogs, went along, and after some extensive shuffling prior to landing with Rattay—a slightly prolonged stay in Virginia, a trip to Best Friends, a transfer to Bad Rap in Oakland, then on to San Diego—he seemed to have regressed from where he'd been in the shelter. Still, Rattay had seen the more confident Iggy, and since she worked from home, giving her plenty of time to devote to him daily, she felt certain he would regain his stride.

But Iggy foundered. He was so crippled with fear that he would not leave the house. "He had no physical scars, but the mental and emotional ones ran deep," Rattay says.

Eventually, though, Rattay gained his trust. To combat his issues she made his world as small as possible, keeping him on a highly regimented routine and limiting his space to the house and the yard. When visitors came over, Rattay would put Iggy in his crate, where he felt safe. He liked her other dogs, Jake and Darla, and he enjoyed meeting the new fosters that sometimes came to stay. Over time he made some progress. He would play with the other dogs and spend a lot of time in the yard, lying in the sun.

He maintained that state for several years, but he'd plateaued, no matter what Rattay tried. Then he started getting worse. "He was happier for a long time, had more good days than bad," Rattay says, "but then he wasn't. That balance shifted, and he was suffering." Lengthy consultations with Donna and Tim at Bad Rap and Rebecca Huss, the dogs' court-appointed guardian, followed, and eventually the group decided that it was in Iggy's best interests to put him down.

Rattay is now an animal control officer in San Diego and although she shuttered Just a Dog, she remains involved in rescue. Iggy, she says, "shows how great the range is on the dogs that came out of this situation. Some went right into foster homes and did great, and some are still at Best Friends. As rescuers we can provide a lot, but we need to remember that they're all individuals and who the dog is plays a part."

As for the time she spent with Iggy, five years filled with highs and lows, she has no regrets. "I wouldn't trade it for anything," she says. "He was amazing. One of his favorite things to do was to roll on his back in the grass. I can still picture him doing that, totally blissed out, and that makes it all worth it."

JHUMPA JONES

With its Sanskrit roots, the name Jhumpa seems right for a dog that starts each day with a canine version of the Sun

Salutations. According to Kathleen Pierce, who rescued Jhumpa when the dog was caught in a torturous mangle of red tape and inferior care for months after leaving the government shelter, Jhumpa has a yogic approach to life. Every morning Jhumpa Jones ambles out the back door and, says Pierce, "the first thing she does is her vinyasa." She starts with a classic downward dog, progresses into an upward dog, then rolls onto her back and shimmies in the grass. "She gets back in touch with the earth," Pierce explains.

That done she sets off on a slow exploration of the yard, probing the perimeter of the nearly one-acre plot, wandering across the grass, and, her favorite, finding a patch of sun to lie in. "She's starting to slow down," says Pierce, who no longer takes the dog for therapy work or to visit schools. "I'm just trying to enjoy her and let her live out her golden hours in peace." Sort of.

It also happens that Jhumpa is the queen bee of a swarm that includes a few cats, two Chihuahuas, and an 18- month-old, 85-pound ball of fire named Biggie Beans. Jhumpa rules the roost with wisdom and forbearance, putting up with a steady flow of silliness and hyperactivity while setting a good example for all. With Beans in particular, another pit bull, she has provided mentorship, tolerating his affronts with an eye roll and the occasional motherly correction.

That's not to say she isn't above a little playfulness of her own. House policy is that when the dogs go out the doggy door, they get a treat every time they come back in the same way. Jhumpa, who loves only one thing more than a good nap in the sun—eating—would sometimes go out through the little door, take two steps, turn around and squeeze back through.

Much as she appreciated that little trick, Pierce had to put a stop to it, if for no other reason than that Jhumpa was diagnosed a few years ago with an intestinal ailment that requires a restricted diet and prednisone treatment.

Otherwise, she's in good health. Still, Pierce can't help but grow reflective. "She's become just a dog to me, which is what I always dreamed of. But seeing the gray in her muzzle, it has reminded me of how incredible the journey has been and how important her voice has been," she says. "So after pulling way back, I got more active again, started posting on her Facebook page more, began talking to the world. It's always humbling to read the comments after those posts because the world is still so moved by these dogs and their victory."

JONNY JUSTICE

A little black-and-white Staffie bull with one pink ear, Jonny Justice always seemed irrepressible, and time has proven that to be true. You just can't keep Jonny Justice down.

Two years ago he lost his housemate, Lily, the pit bull adopters Cris Cohen and Jen Long brought home before Jonny, but Jen now works at home, and when she's travelling, Jonny goes to work with Cohen, where he's been adopted as something of a mascot; there are little Jonny stickers all over the office and his picture is on the company website.

He had double knee surgery in 2015, and there was a complication on one side during healing, leading to another surgery. He was temporarily slowed, for sure, but the recovered Jonny is almost as energetic as ever. "He has a little gray on his face," says Cohen, "and he sleeps a little more, but he's still crazy." Meaning his bursts of hyper zoominess last only five minutes now and his twice-a-day walks are down to a mile or a mile-and-a-half each.

Then there's Jonny's therapy work. For a long time Cohen and Jonny volunteered in the Paws for Tales reading program for kids, but Jonny ran into trouble when one of the libraries in the program attempted to ban pit-bull type dogs. Jonny had never worked at that particular library, but Cohen still attempted to negotiate a compromise. When none could be reached and the Paws for Tales administration refused to step in, Cohen and Jonny resigned in protest.

Would that stop Jonny? No. In 2012 he won an online vote for Most Beautiful Dog, for which the Gund company produced a plush toy in his likeness, and in 2014 he was named the ASPCA Dog of the Year.

The following year, Jonny jumped back in to therapy work, making appearances at a library in downtown San Francisco. He started small, limited to a back room on the fifth floor, but before long he'd charmed both library officials and program participants. He now reports to the library's large children's area on the second floor, a hive of activity and fun that suits him perfectly. "A few weeks ago," says Cohen, "I had one mom tell me, 'That's the longest my son has ever paid attention in one sitting.' "

"When I take out his 'therapy dog' vest and he realizes where we're going, he gets just as excited as ever," Cohen says. "Jonny loves people and he loves life, and I don't expect that will ever change."

LANCE

Lance was one of the most emotionally damaged dogs when he arrived at Best Friends. Months passed before he could even walk on a leash or get in a car, but with dedicated effort by his handlers Lance made some early progress. Then he plateaued.

In an attempt to help him deal with people and the world around him, Lance was allowed to spend much of his time in the Best Friends adoption office, and he loved the cats and dogs he interacted with there. He also grew to love rides on the golf cart, as long as he could lean against the driver and the route didn't change.

One family looking to adopt fell in love with him early on, but they could not bring him home because his anxieties kept him from passing the CGC. Lucky for Lance, they were patient, although after waiting several years they had all but given up. Then, to almost everyone's surprise, in January 2015, Lance passed his test. He was free to go home.

His new family picked him up, and off he went. Five months later, he died in his sleep. "It was very sad," says Best Friends' Michelle Weaver, "but we were all grateful that he got to live in a home with a family who loved him, even if it was just for a little while."

LEO

An early poster boy for the potential that lay in all the Vick dogs, Leo recovered from the trauma of Bad Newz Kennels and government custody faster than any other victim.

Within a few months of moving in with Marthina McClay he had passed his CGC, and less than a year after that he was a certified therapy dog, making regular appearances at hospitals, nursing homes and schools for troubled kids, where he provided companionship and helped educate people about pit bulls and dogfighting.

But by 2011 Leo began to have seizures, and despite the ongoing efforts of McClay, her vet and a veterinary neurologist, his condition worsened over time. By December of that year his health had grown so bad that McClay estimated he was only himself for about an hour a day, and with great sorrow she had him put down. "I want him to be remembered for how beautiful he was," she said at the time.

In the years since, McClay, who runs an organization called Our Pack, has continued to work in dog rescue. She gives talks and offers support at shelters, helping dogs find homes and helping people better care for their pets. For instance, a nearby homeless shelter allowed people to bring dogs, but they had to be spayed or neutered. Most residents weren't in a position to make that happen, so McClay and her group provided the service, allowing families and pets to stay together. "People want to be good owners, but they don't have the resources," she says. "We try to help." These days, she does a lot of work with Chihuahuas, which have overrun the shelters near her home in Northern California that were once filled with pit- bull type dogs.

"That [decrease in the pit-bull shelter population] has been great to see," she says. "And this case, these Vick dogs, really got the ball rolling, showing people that it's not the breed, it's the individual dog. And that's been so important."

LITTLE RED

Susan Weidel had volunteered at Best Friends since 2004, spending one week a year helping out around the grounds. After the Vick dogs arrived she followed the sanctuary's online updates. "One of those posts had a photo of Little Red, and her eyes drew me in," she recalls. She started sponsoring Little Red, giving money to Best Friends meant specifically for the dog's care, and the next time she went to volunteer she worked in the unit where Little Red lived, getting to know the dog. After two such visits Weidel finally decided to put in an application for adoption.

Little Red, who has scars and filed-down teeth, had been a bait dog at Bad Newz Kennels, and she'd been stuck at Best Friends for three years because she could not pass her CGC. Like other adopters, Weidel figured her bid was a long shot; she never imagined she'd be considered worthy. "I thought I'd be laughed out of the place," she says.

She wasn't. Not only that but in August 2011, Little Red passed her CGC. Weidel brought her five other dogs to meet Little Red and she was great with all of them, including Weidel's three-legged Pomeranian, Carl. But once she was in the reality of a home setting Little became freaked out. Enter Cheeto, another of Weidel's dogs, who took Little Red under his wing, showed her around, watched out for her. The two would even curl up together.

Little Red began to adjust, slowly. She was still scared of everything—the appearance of the Christmas tree drove her under the bed for a few hours—but slowly she was working things out. "She was traumatized and she needed to recover," Weidel says. When Weidel would open her door, giving her pack access to her six acres of fenced property, they would all tear out except for Little Red, who'd slowly pick her way around the perimeter of the yard. Open spaces were just too much for her.

Until one day when Cheeto and Little Red were playing along the fence. Suddenly, Cheeto took off across the yard, and Little Red, without thinking, tore off after him—right out into the open. After a moment the dog realized where she was and she peeled off and kept running around. She saw Weidel and charged toward her. "She was so happy she didn't know what to do with herself," Weidel says. As some sort of improvised compromise she ran circles around Weidel and jumped on Cheeto, who looked at Weidel with an expression of shock. That was the beginning of Little Red's emergence from her shell.

Progress proved to be inconsistent, and as Little Red aged new challenges emerged. She was babesia positive, had arthritis and Cushing's disease, and she was blind in one eye. She had cancerous skin tumors removed, and she grew somewhat feeble. Still, she spent her days with Cheeto, who's 17, basking in the sun or the heat of a fire. She also became something of a mother to Weidel's Chihuahua-Jack Russell mix. Her face went white, Weidel says, but her eyes were as compelling as ever.

Sadly, on April 3, 2017, I received the following email from Susan Weidel: "I wanted you to know that Little Red passed away last evening in her sleep. She had a stomach upset earlier in the day and visited her vet for IV fluids and anti-nausea medication. She spent the day at home with me and her pack mates, dozing off and on. She died peacefully in her sleep at 10 p.m. I was at her side as she took her last breath, as were my other dogs. I am in shock and have not yet absorbed the loss of my iconic little dog. She was 14 years old and lived happily in her home for over five-and-a- half years. There are no words...."

LUCAS

The other Grand Champion fighter to come out of Bad Newz Kennels, Lucas was super confident. The staff never tested his compatibility with other dogs, but he could at the least tolerate being in the same room without reacting. People were his thing though, which is why he spent much of his time hanging around the CEO's office at Best Friends, where he could clown with the staff and greet the many visitors.

Lucas's friendliness belied his scarred face and made his happy demeanor all the more endearing. Those scars were also a reminder of why he could never leave Best Friends: the fear, even though he'd been neutered, that dogfighters would try to kidnap him. He struggled on and off with babesia and complications from the disease led to his demise in June 2013. Before that day arrived, his openness and comfort around strangers led to his being one of the most photographed of the Vick dogs and something of a poster boy for why even the most hardened fighters were worth giving a chance. That's what he's remembered for.

MABEL

Like Jhumpa Jones, Mabel went to the Richmond Animal League and was then fostered out to a rescue in upstate New York. She cycled through various homes before settling in with a woman who preferred not to discuss herself or her dog publicly. From the start Mabel had numerous health problems, and these led to her passing about two years after being taken in.

MAKEVELLI

Tattoo artist Brandon Bond's Atlanta Pit Bull rescue took in two of the Vick dogs and Bond personally adopted Makevelli, or Mak as he's called. Since then Bond's life has changed a little: he bought a ranch well outside the city, and he had a son, Remington, who's now four. Both events have had a big impact on Mak's life.

Bond and his family spend about 90 percent of their time at the ranch, with chicks, rabbits, foster dogs, passing deer and an endless supply of scurrying squirrels. "It's like the Island of Misfit Toys," Bond says. "And Mak's the king." His queen is a pit bull named Tsunami and his trusty knight errant is Gatsby, a four-year-old pit bull rescue from Connecticut. When the Bond family does visit the city, the dogs can't wait to get back. The entire ranch is fenced, so as soon as they pull through the front gate, Bond stops and opens the door and the dogs simply take off, running behind the truck all the way to the house.

They often do the same when he opens the house door, piling into the yard to run, play and chase deer. There are balls all around, and if no one will toss one, the dogs pick them up and throw them to themselves. Mak in particular loves to ride the boat on the property's small lake and chase Bond's ATVs around the property, wagging with excitement as soon as Bond opens the garage door.

That's not to say Mak doesn't get his share of rest and relaxation. He takes over the master bedroom, where he sprawls on the bed for hours at a time, and he has a daily routine that he expects to be honored. If it's not he'll shoot the people around him a sideways look that seems to indicate both surprise and disappointment. "He has the cushiest, most spoiled-rotten life of any dog I've ever had," says Bond.

Mak has earned the pampering. He couldn't pass his CGC because he couldn't get past the sound trigger, and his ongoing struggles include a wariness of large men and noises, everything from a soda can popping unexpectedly to the sound of gunfire at a range not far from the ranch.
He's also terrified of the bonfires Bond builds semi- regularly.

He's great with the foster dogs that pass through, though, and helps settle many of them, even those with aggression issues. He's also become buddies with Bond's son. Mak becomes excited when Remington gets home from school, and he'll follow the boy around, playing hoops with him in the driveway or lying on the bed beside Remington while he plays Minecraft.

Bond's first dog, the one that got him started in the rescue world, was a pit bull named Cain, who died a few years ago at the age of 17. When Bond left the house with Cain and the dog did not return, Mak seemed to understand instinctively what had happened. He went over and sniffed Cain's bed, then he approached Bond, licked his face and sat with him for the rest of the day. "I was distraught, and he
helped me out," Bond says. "He got me through a rough day.

MEL

Talk-radio host Richard Hunter gained a bit of viral fame in February 2011 when he attempted to question Michael Vick after a ceremony in Dallas at which the quarterback received the key to the city. Vick rebuffed the effort somewhat dismissively, and the subsequent video of the encounter spread quickly across the Internet.

Hunter had been covering the Vick case on his show from the start, and in 2009 he contacted Best Friends for a segment on the dogs. While he had the sanctuary on the phone, he volunteered to become an adopter when the time came. He wasn't sure if the people he spoke to took him seriously or not, but after nine months passed without a word, he figured they hadn't. Then the phone rang.

Hunter, who was living in Las Vegas at the time, began the application process, and as Best Friends' personnel got to know him, they suggested that Mel might be a good fit. They knew Mel did well with other dogs and they were looking for a home with an older, neutered dog that could serve as a mentor. Hunter's other pup, Pumpkin, a mixed- breed, fit the description exactly, so in March of 2010 Mel went home with Hunter.

It was tough at the start. Like many of the Vick dogs, Mel had his fears. Meeting new people was particularly hard. Sometimes a face-to-face would leave him shaking for as long as 20 minutes, and he couldn't settle down if strangers were in the room. Pumpkin would help by shielding Mel from outsiders, but he could do just so much. The only time Mel felt comfortable around strangers was if they had a dog with them.

Over time, Hunter moved to Texas. Pumpkin died. Two new dogs, Sasha and Halsey, arrived. And Mel improved. Now, he loves to play with other dogs and will even adjust his level of roughhousing depending on how big his playmate is. He sleeps in bed every night, with his head on the pillow, snoring in Hunter's ear. In the morning he goes to the studio with Hunter—Mel doesn't bark—and after work the two head to the gym. Those activities have aided his socialization and though he's still afraid of strangers, Mel can now distinguish between the familiar outsiders he sees around the office and training center and complete unknowns. And when he does meet a stranger, it takes him far less time to acclimate.

In May of 2011 the mayor of Dallas gave out another key to the city. This time it went to Richard Hunter. And Mel.

MERYL

Meryl arrived at Best Friends bearing a court order to spend the entirety of her days there because she bit one dog during the ASPCA's initial evaluations and she bit a handler, although the man did something that was a known trigger for her. Since then she's calmed considerably and has a circle of caregivers who call her Mama Meryl and spend time with her. She has a history of eating things she's not supposed to—toys, beds—but among her favorite things is "pillow time," when one or two of those handlers plop down on a large cushion and she lies and cuddles with them.

Thanks to that sort of enrichment over the years, she's no longer nervous or aggressive when meeting new people, and since 2009 she has lived with another dog, Buddy Arnold, who's her best friend. She's very smart and even took on and enjoyed some agility work before she started to slow down. Now, when she's not playing with Buddy, she likes to lie in the sun and take in the world.

MYA

One of the four dogs still at Best Friends, Mya lives with Curly and the pair spend most of their time hanging around the Dogtown offices of Best Friends. The hope is that spending more time around people will help Mya overcome her lingering fear issues, which have prevented her from passing her CGC.

Besides her fear, Mya has been held back by a more mysterious problem: she's not motivated by food. That oddity knocks the legs out from under normal training protocol, and it has left the Best Friends staff searching for other alternatives to inspire her. So far, none have really worked. "She doesn't really enjoy the training process, so she has a short attention span" says Best Friends' Michelle Weaver. "She's still working on her basics."

That's not to say she doesn't enjoy life, favoring walks, car rides and other dogs and cats. In fact, she's so good with other pooches that she's often assigned to help socialize puppies that arrive at Dogtown. This affinity for canine friends is only Mya's second most endearing quality, the first being her appearance: Her front feet point out, her back legs are bowed and her ears are crooked. "Her body was not well designed," says Weaver, which isn't helping as she has aged and started to grow a bit arthritic. Somehow, though, that all adds to her appeal. Says Weaver, "With people she knows, she's just super sweet."

OLIVER

"The day they announced Michael Vick was eligible to play in the NFL, I lost it," says Erika Sprinkle. "I was so furious. I thought, Karma will get him, but it wasn't helping. The anger was ruining me." Sprinkle knew that sitting around stewing about the injustice would only make things worse. She had to do something about it. She and her husband, David, had been members of Best Friends for years, so she knew the dogs that had gone to the sanctuary were starting to come up for adoption. She called and asked about bringing one of them home, and the application process began.

The NFL made its announcement on July 28, 2009, and by Halloween, Erika, David and their 128-pound German shepherd-husky mix, Boss Man, were on their way from Wichita to Utah to meet Oliver. Upon arriving, the staff suggested that Sprinkle go into Oliver's run alone to start the introductions. She had seen pictures, so she recognized him as soon as he appeared, but she was surprised by one thing: She hadn't expected him to be so small. Maybe 40 pounds, he was short and stocky, mostly black with white front paws and a white racing stripe that ran down his forehead and spread out around his black nose.

He took quickly to Erika and was also happy to meet David and Boss Man. To be sure that everyone got along, the quartet spent the next three days together. That included a trip to Zion National Park, where Boss Man showed that he intended to take Oliver under his wing by teaching the smaller dog to swim in a creek. "From the beginning those two took to each other like two peas in a pod," Sprinkle says.

But Oliver had not yet passed his CGC. Best Friends could send the dog to Erika and David as a foster, but if he didn't pass the test shortly thereafter they would not be able to adopt him. As with all the dogs, a Best Friends trainer would have to make the delivery and go over some basic guidelines for working with Oliver, and the Sprinkles would have to arrange for an approved local trainer to work with the pooch.

The details were worked out and a week before Thanksgiving, Oliver arrived in Kansas, a moment of which Sprinkle says she "has never been more proud." Oliver settled in quickly, reuniting with Boss and making fast friends with the family cat, Squeaky, who ruled the house. The three of them would often sleep together on the couch. At more active times Oliver would launch himself off the front porch like Superman to chase Boss around the yard. And sometimes Squeaky would sneak up on Oliver, swat him on the nose and run, inspiring Oliver to jump up and chase his ambusher around the house.

If Oliver was great with other dogs—and cats—he was a little leery of people. Even as she grew closer to him, Sprinkle noticed that Oliver didn't give kisses. He would nudge her with his nose, but that was about it. Still, they bonded, and if he got nervous around strangers, she could calm him by singing to him. Finally, about a month after he arrived, he laid a wet one on Sprinkle. Then he almost never stopped. Every morning he would lick her legs, a ritual she called "the blessing of the ankles," and he particularly liked to lick the bottoms of people's feet.

As Sprinkle and the trainer continued to work with him and expose him to more people and situations, Oliver became comfortable enough around others that about four months after arriving, he passed his CGC. Erika and David immediately adopted him and threw a party packed with dogs and people to celebrate. Oliver remained a little unsure around strangers, but he had a blast with the dogs.

Ironically, what finally helped him overcome his lingering fears was getting sick. In 2011, Oliver was diagnosed with cancer of the lymph nodes. Once a week, Sprinkle had to leave him at the vet's office for the day so he could receive treatment. Dropping him off was hard, but those afternoons spent without her allowed Oliver to grow confident and comfortable with almost anyone in virtually any situation. The chemo, directed by a panel of experts at Kansas State's veterinary school, took a lot out of him, but within a day or so he would pop up and be back to his old self, running and playing.

Despite the treatment, the cancer would not abate. Over time it spread to his bone marrow and his lungs. By early 2013, Sprinkle could tell he was winding down. After one treatment in early February, Oliver wasn't popping back up. A few days went by and he continued to drag. He seemed to be suffering, and as she watched him one morning Sprinkle knew she would have to take him to be put down that day.

As he lay on the couch with Boss and Squeaky, she leaned over and gave him a hug. Oliver put his head in the crook of her elbow, let out a long breath, and he was gone.

Sprinkle was heartbroken, but she took solace in knowing that he'd died surrounded by love, and that she'd taken her anger and channeled it into something positive and redemptive. It may have only been four years, but, "It was the best thing that ever happened to me," Sprinkle says. "I looked into his eyes every night and told him how beautiful he was."

The Parrots Troop:
RAY, OSCAR, SQUEAKER, and LAYLA

The story of how Ray ended up in the home of Kevin and Jacque Johnson is something of an odyssey that hinges on a handful of other Vick dogs, several Best Friends staffers and an interdepartmental transfer. For years both Kevin and Jacque worked in parrot rescue at Best Friends.

Although the couple toiled in the Parrot Garden or "Parrots," as it's called, they were friends with a Dogtown vet tech named Annick*, who had made Oscar and Squeaker her special projects.

Besides the regular work she and other staffers did with those two dogs, Annick spent her lunch hours and part of her weekends doing extra enrichment with them. Each of the dogs was limited to staff-only contact, but she often took them on car rides, which they loved, and on excursions all over the Best Friends grounds, letting them interact with dogs and horses and whatever else they could find.

These journeys helped, but she also wanted the pair to get exposure to people they didn't know, so she recruited Kevin. Every day at lunch he'd head to Dogtown and provide "stranger danger" for Oscar and Squeaker to deal with. Annick also started bringing the dogs to Parrots once a week, where they'd spend the day in Jacque's office. Many people at Best Friends have office pets, animals that hang out for the day, then return to their pens at night. With squawking birds, noisy office machines and people coming and going, the Parrot Garden offered plenty of chances for the dogs to confront their fears.

Squeaker already got along with people well. Oscar, not so much. He was so scared he wouldn't even come close enough to take a treat out of someone's hand, but spending time in the office was helping him come out of his shell. He was still nervous, and he shut down any time he got stressed, but he was making progress. Having Squeaker around helped; she was more assertive and energetic. He was happy to sit behind her when new people approached and let her take the lead when they made forays into the world.

Squeaker and Oscar were doing so well that they started to spend more time at Parrots. Then, Jacque and Annick convinced Best Friends to add a doggie door to Jacque's office and convert a small, attached greenhouse into an outdoor run so Squeaker and Oscar could live there full time. Squeaker moved in first, but went off to have ACL surgery before Oscar arrived. While she was still recovering, Annick decided she would adopt Squeaker, so the dog never returned to Parrots. On his own, Oscar made himself comfortable. The time in the office, the relative peace, the routine—including daily butt scratches, his favorite—and the work with his handlers allowed him to settle down and pass his CGC. He was adopted shortly thereafter.

That cleared room for Layla to move into Jacque's office. Once again, the reprieve had the desired effect. Layla didn't much care for Dogtown. It's a wonderful place, but there's a lot going on, and for a high-strung dog like Layla, it was difficult to deal with all the stimuli. Spending her days in Parrots helped her calm down.

Kevin and Jacque worked with her as they had Oscar, although Layla had a bigger challenge; she was reactive to other dogs. To help with that problem, Kevin recruited another Best Friends employee, Michele Logan, to join him on weekends taking Layla for long walks with other dogs, helping desensitize her to being around them. Layla never reached a point where she was friendly with strange dogs, but she could tolerate them enough to pass her CGC.

By that time, Kevin and Jacque had spent so much time with Layla and worked so hard with her that they'd grown attached to her. They wanted to put in an application for adoption, but they hesitated because they were unsure how she would get along with their other dogs. By the time they decided to go for it, someone else had beaten them to it.

It had been two years since Kevin first started helping with the dogs and after the success with Layla he was given the opportunity to take on a more formal role at Dogtown. He started splitting his day: half at Parrots and half with the dogs. He was assigned to the part of the compound where Ray lived, and the two hit it off. Besides his regular duties, Kevin would spend a little extra time every day working with Ray and the two grew close.

With Layla gone, Ray became the next dog to move into Jacque's office. Although he was dog-reactive—and had even gotten into a few brief, harmless scuffles—he'd grown contented in Dogtown. His move to the office exposed his lingering troubles. He didn't like loud noises—like squawking birds—and new places, and he was leery of men. Ray couldn't deal with the office and soon returned to Dogtown, but Kevin and Jacque vowed to keep working with him.

"We developed sort of a good-cop, bad-cop thing with him," Kevin says. "I would take him for long walks and not ask much of him, give him lots of treats and lots of affection. Jacque would then work with him on his skills, and she'd push a little harder." After many miles on the trails and sessions with trainers, Ray too passed his CGC.

Kevin and Jacque were determined not to let this one get away. They put in an adoption application, but before they could take him home, they had to find a new house. As a condition of being allowed to take in the Vick dogs, Best Friends promised that it would not allow anyone who lived in Kane County, where the sanctuary sits, to adopt one of them. So Kevin and Jacque found a new home across the border in Arizona, and Ray came to join them.

At Best Friends, Kevin and Ray had developed a deep bond. Kevin recalls one day in particular, when he was asked to show a photographer around Dogtown. Naturally, Kevin took her to see Ray, and he played with the dog as the photographer snapped images. It was around dusk, a time of day when the energy and bustle of the compound begins to naturally settle and a warm desert light permeates. At one point, the photographer pulled her eye away from the camera, looked up at Kevin, and said, "Boy, this dog loves you."

As soon as they got home, though, it became clear that Ray was Jacque's dog. The two became inseparable. He followed her everywhere. They ate together, walked together, played together. They flew together, when Jacque took him to Breed Specific Legislation protests in her native South Dakota. And when Jacque moved into a different part of the Parrot complex, away from the noise of the birds, Ray went to work with her every day.

Part of coming home also meant that Ray had to deal with Kevin and Jacque's three other dogs. Ray got his own room and gates bisected the house to give everyone space without any chance of coming face-to-face, but pretty quickly Ray got into a routine and his fear abated while his trust grew. As always, he loved meeting new people, and Jacque would take him to lunch in the village where he'd charm strangers. In the summer he'd work at Best Friends' summer camp, where he loved romping with kids. Eventually, the Johnsons removed the gates and let all the dogs interact freely, without a problem.

Loud noises still haunted Ray, though. Thunder, car horns, beeping phones. The smoke alarm went off in the house one day, and Ray bolted from the room. When Kevin and Jacque found him, he'd barged into the garage and climbed to the top of a 10-foot-high shelving unit. (Apparently, he climbed when he was afraid. During his weeks in her first office Jacque often found him on top of the desk or the filing cabinet.)

He also battled babesia. Eventually the symptoms became bad enough that Kevin and Jacque could see he was suffering. So 15 months after they brought him home, they decided to follow their vet's advice and have Ray's spleen removed, which often alleviates the discomfort and extends a dog's life. On the day of the surgery, they received a call saying that Ray had come through the procedure in good shape, and he was resting. They looked forward to seeing him the next day, but at 11:00 p.m. the phone rang. Ray had developed a blood clot. It killed him instantly.

Kevin and Jacque were distraught. In the previous year, they'd lost three dogs, and although they'd adopted new ones—Turtle, a fight-bust rescue; Bubba, who was found in a dumpster in Denver with wounds consistent with dogfighting; and Bosco, another fight-ring refugee—none of them could quite fill the space that Ray had occupied in their hearts or defray the feeling of an opportunity lost.

"I wish he would've lived," Kevin said, "because he was just starting to come into his own. He was just starting to be a real dog."

OSCAR

Rachel Johnson wasn't involved in rescue or advocacy. She'd never even had a dog. But in 2012 she decided she was ready to share her life with a four-legged friend. She started poking around a few rescues near her Las Vegas home. The Vick case had passed through her peripheral vision, in headlines and cable news clips, but she hadn't focused on it or spent much time thinking about it.

She had friends who'd had pit bulls, so she knew their bad reputation was undeserved. She also had friends who'd adopted from Best Friends, so she was familiar with the organization. She visited the Best Friends website and saw that a few of the Vick dogs remained available for adoption. She perused their online profiles. She read more about the case.

The more she learned, the more she felt she wanted to help one of those dogs. She kept coming back to two dogs in particular: Ray and Oscar.

Ray seemed like a good candidate, but he wasn't good around strange men, and, as Johnson says, "Being a single woman, I felt as though I'd like the option to have men around." Oscar, well, he was an equal-opportunity scaredy-cat: he was a little uneasy around everyone. Dogs he loved; people made him a nervous.

Johnson put in an application and was accepted. Oscar went home in the middle of 2012, after four years at Best Friends. His reaction to finally making it into a house? Total indifference. He had almost no interest in Johnson.

In truth, he was too busy adjusting to his new surroundings. Any noise jolted him, steps were an obstacle, doors were suspicious. Finally, after a month, he began to realize that his new home was not only safe, but it offered the opportunity for warmth. He began approaching Johnson for pets and those prized butt scratches. Those morphed into chill sessions on the couch and eventually outright cuddling.

Johnson had worked her way into the circle of trust, but

others were still suspicious characters until Oscar got to know them. When strangers arrived Oscar would retreat to Johnson's walk-in closet to hide out, and eventually it became such a place of comfort for him that she put his bed in there.

She also put plush chew toys in there. They were his favorite, not just because he loved to play with them, but because he loved to shred them. Sometimes he'd rip into them immediately, and other times he'd save them for a while before disemboweling. Once, Johnson came home to find a scene that looked like something from a Smurfs snuff movie, with white fluffy stuffing spread across the house. Oscar had gone on a bit of a binge, tearing up a whole troop of fluffy things that he'd saved up for months.

While they were in Vegas they often met up with Mel and Richard Hunter, to go for walks and romps. Mel even stayed over a few times while Richard traveled. But eventually, Rachel and Oscar moved to Colorado, where they lived with Rachel's mom and her dog, a mini dachshund named Molly. She was a confident little thing, a great role model, and Oscar took to Molly immediately. Under her guidance Oscar came out of his shell even more, reaching the point where he'd even approach people. And he found his voice. In the first few years, he never barked, but he started to again.

The improvements were welcome, and Oscar's life largely became that of an ordinary dog, albeit one who preferred a small, quiet existence surrounded by people he knew and familiar turf, spiced with car rides and other dogs. Eventually, time caught up with Oscar, who'd reached 14. In the latter half of 2016 he began to break down both physically and mentally. As his time ticked away, Johnson spoiled him rotten. Then, on January 17, 2017, for the second time in his short life, she set him free.

SQUEAKER

Squeaker isn't at ease with dogs she doesn't know, which is why initially Annick, who has six other dogs, hesitated to adopt her. But when it became clear that Squeaker could adapt when she's introduced properly and has time to adjust,

Annick decided to bring her home.

Squeaker fit into her new pack without a problem. When it comes to people, she's the most affectionate of the group, and she likes nothing better than to cuddle on the couch—as long as she can have at least a paw touching everyone. Finally at home, in a place where people clearly understand her needs and how to work around her difficulties, she's having a great life.

LAYLA

Teresa Rushton jumped in with both—or was it all four?—feet in 2012. She was doing a five-week internship at Best Friends to get certified as a dog trainer and looking for the perfect dog to adopt. While she was at Best Friends the five-year anniversary of the Vick dogs' arrival came around, and part of the celebration was a dog parade. That was the first time Rushton saw Layla, and she soon arranged for a more intimate one-on-one introduction. Within minutes of that meeting Rushton said to herself, "I think this is my dog."

Rushton began to spend time with Layla daily, playing and going for walks, and getting to know her on her turf. She learned about Layla's history, which had its share of rough patches. Layla was, and still is, very dog reactive, and she doesn't like loud noises. Living in the general dog population at Best Friends, surrounded by barking canines, pushed her so far beyond her ability to cope that, as Rushton says, "she could barely think."

Layla began to chill out when she moved to parrots, and with Jacque and Kevin Johnson's help, she eventually passed her CGC. That made her eligible to go home, and Rushton put in an application. Considering Layla's history, Best Friends was particularly interested in finding her a home where she would be an "only child." That and Rushton's already-established relationship with the dog made her a natural fit, and in May of 2013 Layla left Best Friends. Since then, Layla has thrived. As always, she loves people and gets "wiggly and puppylike when she sees new

faces," says Rushton. She's far less amialble with cats and
other dogs. A bunny or a bird can go by and she'll barely
flinch. Rushton's neighbors have cows and a goat, and Layla
pays them no mind. But twice over the years she's been
approached by an off-leash dog and lashed out at each of
them, although she didn't injure either. Rushton and a trainer
spent a lot of time trying to accustom Layla to other dogs,
and she's gotten to a point where she can tolerate them but
not for long.

She's still skittish about sudden noises or movements,
and she's hyper-aware of what's going on around her when
she eats. She's had ACL surgery and a few cancerous tumors
removed and she's getting a little arthritic at 13, but in
general her health is good. Over the years she's even done
appearances with the local SPCA and sheriff, although now
she prefers to spend her time digging in the yard and going
for three or four walks a day, on which there's always a
chance she'll meet someone new.

PIPER

Originally known as Sox, this brown dog with white paws
was the only one to go to Animal Rescue of Tidewater. She
suffered on and off with babesia, but still managed to
become a certified therapy dog who made regular
appearances in her community.

RED and STELLA

Amanda Mouisset was a behaviorist working with the SPCA of
Monterey when the shelter's three Vick refugees—Ginger, Red
and Stella—arrived. She began working with all three and soon
adopted Red. A "stoic and mature" gentleman, Red was good
with people, to whom he would shimmy up and lean on or even
sit on. "He could be very charming," Mouisset says. From the
start, Red got along well with Mouisset's two middle-school
aged daughters, and although he was a little leery of other dogs

at first, he befriended her two: Janie, a pit bull, and Bella, a Lab. Over time, he became neutral to other dogs, largely ignoring them, and Mouisset would use him when trying to acclimate her clients' dogs.

In 2009 Red was diagnosed with mass-cell tumors, which were removed and followed by six months of chemo. It appeared the treatment had worked, until Red started having seizures. More testing found another tumor at the base of his brain and one in the bone marrow of his neck. There was not much left to do except keep him comfortable.

Around the same time Mouisset had started bringing Stella home on occasion, so they could work together more intensely. And about a month after Red passed, in April 2010, she brought Stella home for good.

Stella was quite a contrast to Red. "She's a pistol," Mouisset says. "Lots of personality." She got along well with people and dogs, but her lingering problem was a lack of confidence when meeting new members of either species. Over time, Mouisset got her to feel better about strange dogs, as long as they approached slowly, and to be less stressed by new people, although she also tries to protect Stella from situations in which she has to encounter many unknowns.

Still, she says, Stella has reached a point where, "If you saw her walking out in public, you would never know." That's important because she loves hikes. Perhaps the only thing she loves more is bed, so much so that at bedtime she'll bark until Mouisset picks her up and takes her off to hit the sack.

"Just like with Red," Mouisset says, "it's great to see her be a normal dog and live a great life."

ROSE

Rose arrived at the Animal Farm Foundation in New York with a severe abdominal injury that turned out to be untreatable. During her short stay at AFF the staff made her as comfortable as possible and provided the brief but very real sense of what it meant to be nurtured and loved. And while Rose may not have survived very long, her legacy and the AFF does.

"The good news is that the fight-bust stuff hasn't been a focus for us lately because people now take the dogs," say Bernice Clifford, the group's director of behavior and training and the person who transported Rose from a   shelter in D.C. to Animal Farm. With adoptions for pit bulls and fight dogs less of an issue, AFF has added new programs, one that trains dogs to do assistance work and another that trains police dogs. The organization is also involved with Paws for Purpose, which places dogs inside Riker's Island correctional facility, where inmates learn to train. The program allows the inmates to master a marketable skill while also providing them with companionship. Once the dogs have finished their training, they're taken back and put up for adoption.

Many but not all of the dogs are pit-bull types, but, these days, in Animal Farm's part of the world, many of them have a good chance of finding a home. "Ten years down the road, these dogs are getting opportunities," says Clifford, "and that's great."

SEVEN and CHARLIE

Besides Brandon Bond's Makevelli, the other two dogs that went to Georgia SPCA/All or Nothing Rescue met very different fates. Charlie was adopted by a young couple who moved into a large house with a big yard outside Atlanta. They quickly took to calling him Chuck, and he continues to do well.

A friend of Bond's adopted Seven, and the dog helped the man through a tough emotional time after his friend committed suicide. Although she had fight scars and signs of multiple breedings, Seven was well adjusted and took to training and living in a home quickly. Shortly after the adoption was complete the pair moved to Florida, where, sadly, Seven slipped out of the yard one day and was fatally hit by a car.

The man was devastated. He had saved Seven, and, during his dark period of mourning, she had saved him. It took him a full year to recover. Eventually, though, he knew he wanted another dog and another rescue, but he still needed some separation. He went for a breed that was as different from Seven's as possible. "He got a small dog," says Bond, "one of those ones you can almost fit in your hand." The little guy helped the man move on and a few years later he adopted a second dog. That one was a pit bull.

SHADOW

Susan and Harold* had five dogs, but they'd never had a pit bull, and didn't know anything about the breed other than the rumors and misconceptions that floated in the ether. So when their son Adam showed up one day with a pit bull puppy, Susan's reaction was, "What's the matter with you, bringing this kind of dog into a home with five other dogs?"

Then she picked up the wriggly little thing, and "within 30 seconds I was in love," she says.

That dog, Coco, became "the sweetest, smartest, gentlest dog" she'd ever known. So a few years later, after Adam had taken Coco with him to college and two of their other dogs had passed, Susan and Harold adopted Molly, a pit bull who'd been dumped in South Florida. She too was a great dog.

When the Vick case broke, Susan and Harold had been making annual trips to volunteer at Best Friends for about five years, so they applied to adopt one of the dogs. At first they focused on Little Red, but Best Friends didn't want to place her in a home with another female dog. They shifted their attention to Shadow, who they went to visit in August 2010. He was a problem. As Susan remembers he was down to about 40 pounds, his eyes were slits and he would tremble when approached.

They decided to press on with the process, and in December they returned for a five-day visit along with Molly. When they brought the dogs together Molly walked in as though she owned the place, and Shadow didn't seem to notice. But within a few minutes he was up on his feet and interacting with her. The handlers decided to let the dogs into the outdoor run. Molly took off at a sprint and Shadow followed. Minutes later they were playing in the snow.

That night, Susan and Harold took Shadow back to the hotel with them, where he settled into his crate and quickly fell asleep. During the night, Susan awoke to hear him snarling, growling and yelping in his sleep. "I'd never heard a dog have such nightmares," she says. She opened the crate and stroked his head until he seemed to settle down. This happened a few nights in a row, and during the day, Shadow refused to walk on a leash and they had to carry him out to relieve himself.

Still, they were taken with him, and when the five days were up they had a hard time leaving him, especially Molly who moped and refused to eat for several days.

When Shadow arrived in South Florida a few weeks later, he was happy to be reunited with Susan and Harold and Molly, but the transition proved to be difficult. His fear got the best of him, and he spend most of his time in his crate. When he went out, he didn't seem to care much for the hot, humid weather (not unlike the conditions of southern Virginia). For a while he wouldn't eat much. When he started to eat, he got fat because he wasn't getting much exercise. Susan would often sit next to his crate to comfort him, and he would extend his neck through the open door to rest his head in her lap. She'd pet him and sing "Blackbird."

He made progress, but slowly. He'd been with the couple two years when one day as Harold sat in the living room, Shadow appeared next to him. Without moving, Harold gently stroked the dog's head. Shadow remained for a few minutes before heading back to his crate, but these excursions started to become more frequent. Then everything changed.

Susan, Harold and all their pets, including a horse, Storm, moved to Arizona (which has a drier climate, that looks, feels and smells much more like Best Friends). Almost overnight Shadow became a new dog. He spent hour after hour outside, running and playing with Molly. He was so over his crate that at one point he destroyed it, although Susan replaced it because he still used if for sleeping and taking refuge from his mortal enemy—thunder.

He got down to a fit 66 pounds and became a big cuddler. Still, Shadow and Molly "got into it a few times" Susan says, seemingly because he tried to go into her crate, but the bouts weren't serious: Susan broke them up easily.

Around the beginning of 2017 an unsettling behavioral trend began to emerge. Shadow no longer wanted to go outside during the day, only at night, and seemed to grow wary of men. At one point, he appeared to lunge at a gardener. Susan isn't sure of the cause but she is consulting her vet and a behaviorist and keeping Shadow out of situations that might cause unease.

The flash of aggression is surprising to her because she knows how caring he can be. She has MS, and sometimes she'll fall. When she does, Shadow will stand next to her and allow Susan to use him to pull herself up. She also remembers one day when she and Harold were sitting at the back of the house. Shadow burst in barking and barking. She stood and he started out of the room, looking back and barking at her as he went. She followed him and he continued to watch her and egg her on. When they arrived in the front room, there was Molly, her back legs wedged between couch cushions and unable to move. Shadow ran up to Molly and licked her face. Susan quickly extricated dog from pillows, and Shadow, his work done, curled up and went to sleep.

*Last name withheld upon request.

SWEET JASMINE

The most frequently asked question about *The Lost Dogs* has been, which dog was on the cover? The answer is Jasmine, whose struggle was the book's central storyline. After it came out, to honor Jasmine's legacy, Catalina Stirling, the suburban-Maryland housewife who adopted Jasmine, founded a rescue group of her own, called Jasmine's House. She also got divorced and moved. Amid all the changes, the rescue work wore her down emotionally, and eventually she handed over the reins of Jasmine's House, which is still going strong. She now lives in the D.C. area and teaches art.

SWEET PEA

Mike Wilson first fostered, then adopted Pea back in 2008. A few years later, Wilson's employer was bought out by another company, and his new bosses gave him the opportunity to work from home outside Baltimore. Now Wilson spends every day with Sweet Pea and Bull, a German shepherd-pit bull mix. This has been great for Pea, who struggled with fear from the start. Having Wilson around full-time has helped her cope, especially since it allows him "to keep her world very small."

Part of that strategy includes limiting her exposure to other dogs. About a year after Sweet Pea came to Wilson she bit another dog he then owned. She hasn't had an incident since, but he's careful about how and when she interacts with fellow canines. She's grown comfortable with Bull, and if he falls behind when the three of them go walking, she'll stop and look for him.

Keeping her life controlled in such ways has given her a sense of security that has, ironically, encouraged her to expand her horizons. When she first arrived, she would rarely emerge from her crate. Then she started to feel more comfortable out of the crate but stuck to the corner of one room. Then she expanded to one side of the house.

Now, she loves car rides and long walks outside. In the summer Wilson often takes her to a lake house, where she's an eager canoe passenger and enjoys splashing around in the shallows. When Wilson recently went on vacation, she stayed at his parents' house, and instead of keeping to one room, as she usually had in the past, she moved around the house and sought out the company of people. Those are huge strides. "She used to be far more timid and nervous," explains Wilson. "Now, she likes to be around people more. The majority of the time, she's happy."

That desire to be with others has played out in an unexpected way. A few years ago, much to his surprise, Wilson heard Sweet Pea bark. It was a first. After it happened a few more times, he realized that sometimes she would fall asleep, and, especially since she'd begun to lose her hearing, wake up and wonder if she were alone in the house. "She was checking in with me. She wanted to know where I was," he says. "It turns out she has a good voice, not piercing or annoying. It has been nice to hear."

TEDDLES

If one trend has marked the recent years for Teddles and his adopter Cindy Houser, it has been health problems met with resilience, for both canine and human. Several years ago, doctors discovered a three-pound tumor near Houser's spine. After surgery to remove it, she was bedridden for months and eventually had to relearn to walk. During the toughest times, Teddles, and his playmate, a pit bull named Izzy, gave Houser the motivation to get out of bed and keep trying. As for Ted, he got his CGC, enjoyed participating in scent-search competitions and spent time visiting special- needs kids (after he was turned down because of a VA hospital's no pit-bull policy), until his health started to decline. These days he still does some nose work in the yard, but he's almost completely deaf, he has mass-cell cancer (which Houser treats holistically) and he's got a heart condition that causes him to pass out if he gets too worked up. That means he can't really take part in any active play or much running. If he does he'll lose consciousness, which one day he won't regain.

Houser tries to avoid situations that will raise his energy or excitement, although that doesn't keep him from his long-time favorite activity: eating. "He's happy," Houser says. "He still loves to walk. He's eating well. He's been a wonderful house dog."

Epilogue: Days after writing about Teddles I received word that he'd passed away. I emailed Houser, who sent back this reply on April 16, 2017: "I miss T-Mac so much, he was the most forgiving creature I have ever known and feel so blessed to have been his forever Mom. Through all my health woes, Teddles was my rock. My last tumor surgery he gave me a reason to get up and walk again. He will always be my hero. I think Teddles actually rescued me!"

UBA

A small black-and-white bundle of energy, Uba was one of the first Vick dogs to find a home, landing with long-time Bad Rap volunteer Letti DeLittle in late 2007. From the start he was functional among the human world if a little skittish, particularly around men. Sure enough, the first time I met him, in a parking lot while attending a Bad Rap training session in Oakland, he growled at me as I approached. But as soon as I turned sideways and took a less direct path toward him, he settled down and let me come say hi. After that, we were fast friends. On a subsequent visit to the Bay Area he jumped on a couch and sat next to me, and even sat in my lap for about 15 minutes while I did a TV interview. This, according to DeLittle, was sort of a big deal.

These days, Uba is more social. He and DeLittle moved east a few years ago and started doing scent work. Uba's not terribly competitive at it, but the game changed his world. During an event, the handler has no idea where the scent is or how to find it, so the dog is in charge. Uba knows that DeLittle's paying attention to his every move and that if he succeeds he'll be rewarded. That dynamic has made him more confident, to the point that DeLittle can now take him on school visits; in the past, "he would have just collapsed," she says.

He's also become a mentor to a number of fight-bust refugees that DeLittle has fostered over the years, helping the dogs settle down and adjust to life in a house. "He's becoming more of a mature gentleman," DeLittle says, which includes getting more chatty and opinionated, sharing his likes and dislikes through squeaks and moans and grumbles. After three knee surgeries he's a little arthritic, which means he needs a lift when he wants to get on or off the couch, a desire he does not hesitate to verbalize.

DeLittle is quick to point out that Uba hasn't slowed *too* much though. "He still has that zest for life," she says, noting that he wears out the doggy door coming and going throughout the day. "He's not perfect, and it hasn't always been easy for him," Delittle says, "but I like to say, he's the best Uba he can be."

WILLIE BOY

Willie Boy arrived at Best Friends seeming sweet and fun-loving but regressed in the early days, at times lashing out and showing a complete inability to be around other dogs. He has improved since then, but as Best Friends Michelle Weaver says, "He still has behavior issues." As was suspected at the outset, at least part of Willie's problems are related to physical discomfort. He has babesia, for which his spleen has been removed, he has had a few cancerous tumors removed, and he has a digestive condition that requires he only get a specified amount of protein.

A dedicated group of handlers are aware of his range of needs—both physical and emotional—and knows how to tend to them. They meet regularly to make and carefully apportion his food, they provide an unwavering routine—since even the slightest variation can throw him off—and they know how to reassure him.

Thanks to these efforts, Willie can feel more at ease, comfortable and relaxed, which allows his old self to resurface. He can even walk with some other dogs now, as long as they mind their manners and he has one of his beloved circle of caregivers close by. But his trauma was such that he'll likely never be a house dog.

ZIPPY

A little ball of energy and mischief, Zippy was one of the stars of the original *Sports Illustrated* story about the dogs, perhaps best remembered for offering her signature greeting when a photographer and I visited: She peed on the floor. Ten years later, adopter Berenice Hernandez reports that Zippy has a little gray in her beard, but she hasn't slowed down.

Crash, the big 70-pound "bundle of love" pittie that she took in around the same time as Zippy, has slowed down. Another foster, a 14-year-old pit bull, has slowed down. But even after ACL surgery four years ago, Zippy is "an older dog with a puppy's brain."

She table- and counter-surfs. She plays with the neighborhood kids. She barks at squirrels through the window and has had run-ins with raccoons and possums in the yard. In the morning, when Hernandez is getting her four kids ready for school, Zippy is her steadfast assistant, at her side every step of the way and ready to clean up any accidents that occur during lunch preparation. If Zippy slacks off it's to watch Hernandez's middle-school son eat his daily waffle. If he steps away from the table, she snatches it.

This is not the only thievery she's known to pursue. She has figured out how to open the dog food canister, and if her meal isn't served right on time, she'll pop the container open and help herself. Only two things slow Zippy down: the large hill near her home, which gets her huffing and puffing a little, and garbage trucks, which continue to baffle and frighten her.

Hernandez too continues at an impressive pace. Besides the four kids, three dogs and job, she still volunteers for Bad Rap, working in its outreach and spay- and-neuter programs. Her husband, Jesse, an animator, even painted Bad Rap's mobile spay-and-neuter van, elegantly dubbed The Nut Truck.

Sometimes, Hernandez will sing "Zip-a-Dee-Doo-Dah" to

her roughly 11-year old pet, but not too often. Hearing the song gets Zippy excited. And even all these years later, when Zippy gets excited, she pees on the floor.

• • •

PART III
The People

JIM KNORR

The onetime USDA agent who helped make the Vick investigation a federal case—a turning point in its successful prosecution—is enjoying his retirement from investigative work. Although he spends time with his grandkids, follows his beloved Maryland Terrapins and plays a lot of golf, he also continues to give back.

He's on the board of directors of Unchained America (unchainedamerica.net), a national group that identifies dogs that live largely outdoors and/or on chains and attempts to get the owners to give them up. In cases where members see signs of neglect or abuse, they'll involve law enforcement. The goal is to adopt the dogs out to more hospitable homes.

Knorr is also on the board of the Salute Military Golf Association (smga.org), which provides "rehabilitative golf experiences" to post-9/11 wounded veterans. The group started with two chapters six years ago and has spread to 11 across the country, all of it run by two staffers working out of an office Knorr secured in the basement of a club where he often plays. To date, SMGA has helped more than 3,000 veterans suffering with everything from PTSD and traumatic brain injury to amputation get lessons, clubs and days out on the course. The USDA has gotten much smaller since he left and all the people he knew have moved on, so he doesn't have much sense of the agency's ongoing involvement in dogfighting. Still, he feels good about his involvement in the Vick case. "It was the best thing that ever happened as far as bringing awareness to dogfighting," he says. "The next step is to educate the public, especially young kids, so we can stop it before it starts."

BILL BRINKMAN

The Surry County detective who led the initial raid on Bad Newz Kennels and persuaded Jim Knorr to involve the Federal government lost his job months after the verdict came down. He continues to spend most of his time in Afghanistan, where he helps train police officers.

STEPHEN ZAWISTOWSKI

After 26 years at the ASPCA, Zawistowski retired in June 2015. As the association's chief scientist, Dr. Z led the government evaluation team and championed the idea of individual assessments for all the dogs. Since quitting his day job, he has moved to a home in southern Michigan overlooking a lake, where he spends his days eyeing up deer, wild turkeys and eagles, among other resident critters. This location also provides him the opportunity to interact with another enchanting form of wildlife: his grandkids.

REBECCA HUSS

The court-appointed special master/guardian of the dogs from Bad Newz Kennels remains a law professor at Valparaiso University. Although she has always focused on animal law, the thrust of her research has changed a bit. Before her involvement in the Vick case she wrote more about the minutia of rescue organizations—their non-profit status and relationship with law enforcement. Since the case she has concentrated more on the ways in which animals impact our lives, specifically the role and value of service and companion animals. In between she's made a variety of presentations and appeared on panels to discuss the Vick dogs, and her latest work is the most directly related to her experiences with that case: In 2016 she published a paper on breed-specific legislation, and by the end of 2017 she expects to have another out on dog forfeiture.

Away from the office, Huss, who lost her mini-dachshund during the Vick court proceedings, has adopted two new dogs of the same breed, Rose and Lilly. She has also become a foster home for the same rescue from which she got her new pooches. Although her official involvement in the Vick case ended when the dogs went to the rescue groups, she does keep abreast of what's happening with them and hears regularly from a cross-section of the adopters and rescuers. Looking back, she relishes the wider impact of the case on dogfighting. "We know it changed the paradigm," she says. "Prosecutions went up, and the last states that had not made it a felony now have."

Just as satisfying, if not more so, is the impact on those specific dogs. "I think," she says, "it's so great for any of them to get into homes and be loved, even if it's just for a few years."

● ● ●

PART IV
The Aftermath

So where does that leave us? What have we learned, what have we gained? Ten years down the road, what does the entire Vick case mean?

All the things that were true at the end of *The Lost Dogs* remain so. The approach of evaluating each dog individually has become the standard, adopted by the Humane Society of the U.S. and almost every precinct and shelter across the country. There is now a federal dogfighting law, and for the first time the practice is considered a felony in all 50 states. Law enforcement continues to find dogfighting to be a gateway crime, and busts of fighting rings usually turn up defendants who are also guilty of drugs and weapons offenses.

And the perception of pit-bull type dogs has changed dramatically. "They were seen as victims, the first [fighting dogs] viewed that way," says Nicole Rattay, the animal-control officer in San Diego who adopted Iggy. Pit-bull type dogs are still the number-one shelter dog, but adoptions are up. ASPCA data collected from 45 shelters spread around the country showed that in 2014 (the last year for which stats are available) intake of dogs identified as bully breeds was down 10 percent, and those dogs rose to second in adoptions. They were still euthanized more than any other breed, but those were down 17 percent.

"People love pit bulls," says Marthina McClay, who adopted Leo and runs Our Pack, a rescue in Los Gatos, California. "We put them up on the website, and people want them. That's because of the Vick case. It started that."

In Atlanta, Makevelli's adopter, Brandon Bond, continues to operate his All or Nothing Rescue, and says that when he posts a pit bull for adoption, he "usually gets three or four applications the same day rather than waiting months like we used to." Such anecdotal evidence extends to Bangall, New York, where the pit bull adoption boom has caused the Animal Farm Foundation to adapt its mission. "In the past year we've expanded the focus of what we do—because so many people are taking the dogs, that we're offering not just adoptions but various kinds of assistance," says AFF's director of behavior and training, Bernice Clifford. "We're providing training, spay and neuter, we've even worked one-on-one with people who wanted to give their dogs up, helping them overcome the problems that made them want to do that."

Bad Rap, the San Francisco pit bull rescue that in many ways was at the heart of the Bad Newz case, has seen similar improvements. "The Vick case has helped things for the better," says Donna Reynolds, who cofounded and runs Bad Rap with her husband, Tim Racer. "There's a generation coming of age that doesn't remember when pit bulls were considered bad. The dogs have captured their hearts."

"In general I'm honored to have taken the journey," says Michelle Weaver, the director of enrichment at Best Friends. "The Vick dogs allowed people to be open-minded about these dogs and give them a chance."

That impact can't be overstated. "They were America's dogs," says Molly Gibb, who adopted Alf, "part of our collective consciousness." The chord these dogs struck, the way the country responded to their plight, condemned the cruelty they suffered and rallied to their defense changed not only the way people view pit bulls but highlighted the expectations people have for our society: Compassion does not trickle down, it bubbles up.

• • •

The campaign against dogfighting remains something of a mixed bag.

In the decade since the raid at 1915 Moonlight Road there have been hundreds of busts of small, back-yard operations and take downs of numerous wide-ranging rings. In 2009 authorities broke open a case that became known as the Missouri 500, a ring based in St. Louis that spread across five states, involved more than 500 dogs and led to 26 arrests. The Alabama 350, taken down in 2013, swept up 367 dogs in multiple states. There was the North Carolina 150 in 2016, and so on.

"In the context of the Michael Vick case, when that first happened people were not really aware of dog fighting. For many it was their first exposure," says Tim Rickey, the ASPCA's

VP of field operations, who along with a team of 19 helps federal and local authorities across the country investigate animal cruelty cases. "Since then, we've seen much more aggressive law enforcement. We're involved in a number of cases at any given time."

Those large-scale busts have slowed to a trickle, though. According to the Humane Society of the U.S., "Most of the big operators have moved to Mexico," says Donna Reynolds. The experts attribute the move to the increased law enforcement and penalties. One of the defendants in the Alabama bust received an eight-year jail sentence, the longest ever in a federal dogfighting case. And in late April 2017, Mexico passed a federal law making dogfighting a felony, so it should get tougher for practitioners south of the border as well.

Still, there are large rings and small operators out there. "At the big Alabama bust we found documented fights with single bets of $250,000," says Rickey. "As long as it's that lucrative it's going to remain prevalent. We're still far from beating it."

In 2016 the FBI began tracking animal cruelty crimes, which means more accurate reporting will be possible in the years ahead, giving authorities a way to quantify the scope of the problem and any progress. That data will be important for helping communities continue to justify the costs.

"The overall challenge is a matter of resources," says Dr. Stephen Zawistowski, the ASPCA's now-retired executive VP and science director. "The struggle for a lot of these groups, the local humane societies, is the money. It's not only the medical care and training, it's the housing while they're being held as evidence."

And the difficulties extend to the courtroom once a case reaches trial. "The sophistication of the [Vick] prosecution upped the game," Zawistowski adds. "Juries now expect analysis of scars and DNA evidence, but often the only thing prosecutors in smaller jurisdictions can offer are breeding charts, break sticks and betting ledgers."

Still, Rickey sees progress, even on the core issues. He estimates that he and his team conduct a training session with a law enforcement outfit every two weeks, explaining to officers around the country how to spot dogfighting, what tools and resources they need and how to approach the cases. The team also focuses on educating both politicians and the public.

"We've dramatically changed our overall approach, and we've seen many cases with multi-agency support, which is 180 degrees from what it was," says Zawistowski. "Certainly all those changes are for the better. It's more than we hoped for. Although in some ways, it's less than we asked for."

● ● ●

What Zawistowski asked for was more data.

The ASPCA's original discussions with the USDA and the Department of Justice about saving the Vick dogs included a request that any rescue groups or individual adopters who took on any of the dogs would provide regular follow-ups in the way of questionnaires and progress reports. The ASPCA even created an online evaluation form for the dog caretakers to fill out and submit. It went unused.

"It's the thing I regret most," says Zawistowski, who also points out that he no longer speaks for the ASPCA. "We've heard a lot of success stories, but we don't know about the others. You can learn just as much from them. What did you try? What worked? What are the trends?"

At Best Friends, Dr. Frank McMillan, a behaviorist, had a similar impulse. He had caretakers at the facility monitor the dogs and fill out daily evaluations of their state of being, rating them on such factors as calmness, sociability and happiness, among others. His hope was to track progress and techniques and learn more about how to deal with such dogs in the future. But this work stopped after a less than a year because the dogs began to move into homes and other parts of the Best Friends facility.

As much as Zawistowski laments the missed opportunity, he's also realistic about what might have resulted from the feedback. "We said at the time that these were not all typical fighting dogs— I don't know if everyone heard that but we said it—so we can't say that they represent how all rescued fighting dogs will be. In many ways these dogs were more like dogs from hoarding cases."

It's true. There were a number of dogs that didn't seem to fit the typical profile of fight-bust survivors. Big, lumbering lugs like Ernie and Teddles were oddballs, as was little Oliver, who

Michelle Weaver first thought was a Boston Terrier. Jonny Justice is a Staffordshire bull terrier who never seemed to direct any ill will toward anything. There was a group of reddish dogs with pink noses that, for the most part, presented as rather docile.

At the same time, Vick did have two documented Grand Champions, Lucas and Georgia, both of whom had caramel brown bodies with black snouts. It makes sense that the Bad Newz brain trust would have bred the pair, and there is a group of dogs with similar coloring that could be the result of such a coupling: Ellen, Handsome Dan, Hector, Layla, Leo, Makevelli, Meryl, Oscar, Ray, Squeaker, and Tug (although Ellen and Dan were a shade lighter). Many of those dogs bore scars from fighting or displayed reactivity to other dogs.

The good news is that almost all of these dogs made significant progress. Some, like Hector and Dan, were almost instantly at ease among fellow canines, while others became at least tolerant of other dogs. Even Lucas and Georgia reached a point where they could spend time with or around other dogs.

Many of the others, the ones more marked by fear of either dogs or people than any sort of aggression, also showed great progress. A number adapted almost seamlessly, moving into homes with people and pooches. Others took longer to adjust but have gone on to live so well, that in the words of their adopters, "No one would know there was anything different about them." A handful faced a continual struggle.

"The Vick dogs represent a spectrum," says Rattay. "Some of them went right into homes, some are still at Best Friends and some are struggling."

Zawistowski would like to know why, to plumb the differences in starting point, stimuli, environment, training, treatment and enrichment, but even for a trained scientist, that missed chance does not diminish the larger accomplishment. "My elevator speech?" says Zawistowski. "This has been a great success that's changed the way we think about and approach these dogs, but I wish we could have followed up and we must stay realistic."

• • •

Keeping it real has become harder than ever. And to a degree, that too is a legacy of the Vick dogs. Rescuing pit bulls is "way easier now," says Brandon Bond. "*The Lost Dogs*, *Pit Boss* and *Pit Bulls and Parolees* did great things. The stigma is a lot better."

The flip side of that progress is more expectations. "Sometimes the Vick dogs gave people a false sense of how many could be saved," says Zawistowski. The truth is, not all dogs can or should be placed in a home.

"Adoption is a service to the community," says Animal Farm's Clifford, "and placing dogs that are not going to do well or that will be a danger to people or animals is not doing anyone a service."

From the start, the larger point of the Bad Newz experiment was not that all dogs should be saved, but that each dog deserved an individual assessment and the opportunity to be placed in a home based on who he or she was, not according to breed or background. "We can't get too emotionally involved," says the ASPCA's Rickey. "We want to be sure any dog we put in a home can be an ambassador for the breed."

That is not always the case these days. "I have seen a lot of people being over aggressive [in pulling dogs out of shelters]," says Bond. "It used to be that rescuers were more hard core. They were in the shelters, meeting the dogs, working with them. Now, there are a lot of people just pulling dogs through the Web and posting them on Facebook. In some ways that's good. In some ways it's not."

The zero-kill movement represents an admirable ideal, but it doesn't always align with the needs of the dogs or the situation. "To me, there are worse things than euthanasia," says Rattay. "In my opinion, it's not right to keep a dog alive to put our feelings above theirs. It's not fair to put a dog in a pen indefinitely just to keep a low euthanasia rate. We do see a lot of people with good intentions, but they ignore who the dog is. The Vick experience helped inform us about what's possible. It was clear that as rescuers we can provide a lot, but who the dog is plays a part, and you can't fix everything."

"Everyone wants to get the dogs out of the shelters," adds Bad Rap's Reynolds, "but we have to figure out why they're in the shelters in the first place." Like other rescue organizations, hers has shifted to helping people keep their dogs. "If these dogs are being euthanized it's not because people don't want them. It's because people are being pushed out of their homes. We're trying to address that." The problems that dog owners face as they downsize include lack of space, apartment buildings that won't allow the breed, resistance from insurance companies and even "no-dog" policies at public shelters. Says Reynolds, "We're touching a different part of the elephant."

· · ·

"Some [of the dogs] will end up with something resembling a normal life, but the chances are very slim, and it's not a good risk to take." This is what a PETA spokesperson told me when I wrote that original article about the dogs for *Sports Illustrated* in December 2008.

So what's the math? What are the actual numbers? Fifty- two pit-bull type dogs were taken off the Vick property. Two died while in government custody, leaving 50 to be evaluated by the teams from the ASPCA and Bad Rap. Of those, two were deemed to be in severe physical or emotional-mental pain and euthanized. The remaining 48 were split up: 22 went to Best Friends, 10 to Bad Rap and the other 15 dispersed in groups of two or three, with a few singles as well.

Since then, at least 17 have passed their CGC, seven were certified as therapy dogs and more than half have made public appearances to support anti-breed legislation or to raise awareness and fight discrimination. At least that many have also been used in training programs and foster homes to act as role models and help calm other dogs.

The majority—37—have lived in a home for at least a few months. Thirteen of the Best Friends dogs found families; four are still there and five died at the sanctuary. As of late April 2017, 24 of the 48 have passed away, including three—Little Red, Teddles and Audie—in the weeks prior to publication.

So was it "a good risk?" Were the government officials, ASPCA scientists and rescuers right to take a chance on these dogs?

"It has been amazing watching them grow, get comfortable and go home," says Weaver, who has worked with the Vick dogs at Best Friends since their arrival. "At the time I was so focused on working with them that it wasn't until later that I saw the impact. They demonstrated that they deserved a chance, and that they should not be judged solely on where they came from."

"It was definitely worth the effort," says Zawistowski. "More than anything we were able to change the conversation about dogfighting, and the dogs. We did learn a lot from the effort, and that education is now being used in new cases. I don't think this would have happened if the dogs were all euthanized at the conclusion of the Vick case."

Those advances shouldn't be taken for granted. As much as things have gotten better for the breed and worse for dogfighters, the atmosphere has changed a lot in the 10 years since the lost dogs were found. It's hard to imagine that if the Vick case was unfolding today, the dogs would be given the same chance that they were in 2007.

That's all the more reason to appreciate the willingness of administrators, prosecutors, judges and legislators to look past the myths and half-truths—to consider the facts, however unpopular. If not for that courage and foresight, the refugees from Bad Newz Kennels never would have been given a chance. As the dogs showed us—and continue to prove— accepting the state of things as they actually are and forging on in the face of those realities is the only way to make progress and create a new, better reality.

• • •